Y6
Hu
experimenta

D0070525

AUG 2 5 2009

At Issue

Human Embryo
Experimentation

Other Books in the At Issue Series:

At Issue

Human Embryo Experimentation

David Haugen and Susan Musser, Book Editors

GREENHAVEN PRESS

An imprint of Thomson Gale, a part of The Thomson Corporation

THOMSON
™
GALE

Detroit • New York • San Francisco • New Haven, Conn. • Waterville, Maine • London

THOMSON

* ™

GALE

Christine Nasso, *Publisher*
Elizabeth Des Chenes, *Managing Editor*

© 2007 Thomson Gale, a part of The Thomson Corporation.

Thomson and Star logo are trademarks and Gale and Greenhaven Press are registered trademarks used herein under license.

For more information, contact:
Greenhaven Press
27500 Drake Rd.
Farmington Hills, MI 48331-3535
Or you can visit our Internet site at http://www.gale.com

LIBRARY OF CONGRESS CATALOGING-IN-PUBLICATION DATA

Human embryo experimentation / David Haugen and Susan Musser, book editors.
    p. cm. -- (At issue)
  Includes bibliographical references and index.
  ISBN-13: 978-0-7377-3243-6 (hardcover)
  ISBN-13: 978-0-7377-3244-3 (pbk.)
  1. Embryonic stem cells--Juvenile literature. 2. Embryonic stem cells--Research--Juvenile literature. 3. Embryonic stem cells--Research--Moral and ethical aspects--Juvenile literature. I. Haugen, David M., 1969- II. Musser, Susan.
   QH588.S83H83 2007
   616'.02774--dc22

                                                        2007006073

ISBN-10: 0-7377-3243-1 (hardcover)
ISBN-10: 0-7377-3244-X (pbk.)

Printed in the United States of America
10 9 8 7 6 5 4 3 2 1

Contents

Introduction

On July 19, 2006, President George W. Bush used his executive veto privilege to reject a piece of legislation entitled the Stem Cell Research Enhancement Act of 2005. The bill, which had won approval in the Senate on the previous day, would have amended the Public Health Service Act to permit federal funding of stem cell research on human embryos discarded by fertility clinics. In applying his veto, the president said, "If this bill were to become law, American taxpayers for the first time in our history would be compelled to fund the deliberate destruction of human embryos. Crossing this line would be a grave mistake and would needlessly encourage a conflict between science and ethics that can only do damage to both and harm our nation as a whole."

President Bush had already made his position on stem cell research clear in August 2001, when he announced that his administration would tolerate funding of adult stem cell research as well as research conducted on roughly 60 strains of embryonic stem cells that had begun before his new policy took effect. No federal funds, however, would be spent in support of new embryo research. Explaining this decision, President Bush said in a televised address, "I . . . believe human life is a sacred gift from our Creator. I worry about a culture that devalues life, and believe as your President I have an important obligation to foster and encourage respect for life in America and throughout the world. And while we're all hopeful about the potential of this research, no one can be certain that the science will live up to the hope it has generated."

The president's assertion that stem cell research is in its early stages is an important facet of the controversy surrounding this science. Embryonic stem cells are taken from five- to six-day-old embryos left over from reproduction techniques such as in vitro fertilization. These cells differ from their adult counterparts because embryonic stem cells can be cultured to produce specific kinds of cells—such as muscle cells or brain cells—through cell division. The offspring of these stem cells include a copy of the original stem cell as well as another cell that has the potential to become any of the more than 200 types of cells in the body. The copy would be retained for further divisions while the more specific progeny would be used in medical therapy.

Advocates of stem cell research anticipate that embryonic stem cells could therefore be used to generate replacements for damaged or diseased cells that are responsible for a variety of human ailments including heart failure and Alzheimer's disease. The replacements would be reinserted into the body to take over the roles of diseased cells of their type. Such therapies have been tried with mice, rats, and other animals with some success. Doctor Su-Chun Zhang of the University of Wisconsin attested in 2004:

> Studies in diseased animal models have begun to show that . . . specialized cells produced from human ES [embryonic stem] cells may be useful in treating certain diseases. Transplantation of human ES cell derivatives into the spinal cord of rats suffering from motor neuron disease promotes the restoration of movement. . . . Cardiac muscle cells, produced from human ES cells, appear to repair infarcted swine heart tissue following transplantation into the infarct area. Dopamine nerve cells generated from nonhuman primate ES cells contribute to functional recovery of Parkinsonian monkeys [i.e., monkeys with Parkinson's disease].

Some research involving animals, however, has produced negative side effects. In one study, embryonic stem cell injections caused brain tumors in mice suffering from Parkinson's disease. While encouraged by the positive progress of embryonic stem cell experiments in animals, most researchers agree that the advances are limited because no one is sure what effects transplanted cells will have on humans.

Although the unknown risks of embryonic stem cell research inform part of President Bush's veto of new experiments in this field, his main contention is moral. To gather stem cells from human embryos, the embryos must be destroyed. The president asserts that his religious convictions coupled with his duty as the ethical figurehead of the nation persuade him to reject science that he believes dismisses the value of life. David Prentice, a professor of life sciences at Indiana State University, made this moral objection clear when he told *National Review* Online, "It has never been acceptable to sacrifice one set of human lives for the potential benefit of others (and they are only potential benefits at this point). Human embryonic stem cell research assigns different values to different human beings, designating some as people and some as property."

Those who debate this view cannot deny that culling stem cells from embryos results in the termination of the embryos. However, some reject the notion that the cluster of embryonic cells is a human life with the same rights as fully formed people. Others follow this somewhat utilitarian view by arguing that medical science should not ignore the right to life of those people already living and yet suffering from debilitating and perhaps ultimately fatal diseases and disorders that might be cured by embryonic stem cell therapies.

Both the contested benefits of this unproven science and the moral concerns over its implementation are discussed in *At Issue: Human Embryo Experimentation*. Although the authors in this anthology see the relief of human suffering as the worthwhile goal of medical experimentation, not all believe the ends justify the means. Some of these commentators contend that harvesting stem cells from a group of cells does not entail the killing of a human life; others believe that all life— even in its most nascent stages—is worth protecting and therefore cannot be sacrificed even for humanitarian purposes. Siding with either viewpoint is a matter of personal conviction.

As Louis Guenin of the International Society for Stem Cell Research rightly concludes, "There is no test for whether an embryo is a person. Instead we are left to our own devices, to our own moral reasoning." And these individual, reasoned and moral decisions will ultimately determine the fate of embryonic stem cell research in the United States.

1

Human Embryonic Research Is Necessary

Terry Devitt

Terry Devitt is the science editor for the University of Wisconsin-Madison's Office of University Relations and the editor for The Why Files, *a Web site presenting topical science issues and news. He has written extensively on the stem cell research taking place at the University of Wisconsin, the place where the first embryonic stem cells were isolated in 1998.*

Embryonic stem cells are the building blocks of human life. They are pluripotent, meaning that they have the potential to develop into any type of adult cell. This ability has led scientists to believe that these cells can be implanted alongside diseased cells and take over the functions of those that do not behave normally. Stem cells can also be used to examine the effects of drugs and chemicals on the body. Furthermore, studying stem cells provides researchers a unique opportunity to examine human development at its earliest stages, a time frame that is poorly understood at present. Only through continued research and increased funding will embryonic stem cells yield all their promise for humanity.

Embryonic stem cells are undifferentiated cells that are unlike any specific adult cell. However, they have the ability to form any adult cell. Because undifferentiated embryonic stem cells can proliferate indefinitely in culture, they could

Terry Devitt, "Stem Cell Basics." *Embryonic Stem Cells: Research at the University of Wisconsin-Madison,* 2000. Copyright © 2006 The Board of Regents of the University of Wisconsin System. Reproduced by permission of the author.

potentially provide an unlimited source of specific, clinically important adult cells such as bone, muscle, liver or blood cells.

Stem Cells from Surplus Embryos

Human embryonic stem cells are derived from fertilized embryos less than a week old. Using 14 blastocysts obtained from donated, surplus embryos produced by in vitro fertilization, a group of UW-Madison developmental biologists led by James Thomson established five independent stem cell lines in November 1998. This was the first time human embryonic stem cells had been successfully isolated and cultured.

The cell lines were capable of prolonged, undifferentiated proliferation in culture and yet maintained the ability to develop into a variety of specific cell types, including neural, gut, muscle, bone and cartilage cells.

The embryos used in the work at UW-Madison were originally produced to treat infertility and were donated specially for this project with the informed consent of donor couples who no longer wanted the embryos for implantation.

In virtually every in vitro fertilization clinic in the world, surplus embryos are discarded if they are not donated to help other infertile couples or for research. The research protocols were reviewed and approved by a UW-Madison Institutional Review Board, a panel of scientists and medical ethicists who oversee such work.

Embryonic Stem Cells Provide Unique Research Opportunities

Embryonic stem cells are of great interest to medicine and science because of their ability to develop into virtually any other cell made by the human body. In theory, if stem cells can be grown and their development directed in culture, it would be possible to grow cells of medical importance such as bone marrow, neural tissue or muscle.

The first potential applications of human embryonic stem cell technology may be in the area of drug discovery. The ability to grow pure populations of specific cell types offers a proving ground for chemical compounds that may have medical importance. Treating specific cell types with chemicals and measuring their response offers a short-cut to sort out chemicals that can be used to treat the diseases that involve those specific cell types. Stem cell technology, therefore, would permit the rapid screening of hundreds of thousands of chemicals that must now be tested through much more time-consuming processes.

The study of human development also benefits from embryonic stem cell research. The earliest stages of human development have been difficult or impossible to study. Human embryonic stem cells offer insights into developmental events that cannot be studied directly in humans in utero or fully understood through the use of animal models. Understanding the events that occur at the first stages of development has potential clinical significance for preventing or treating birth defects, infertility and pregnancy loss. A thorough knowledge of normal development could ultimately allow the prevention or treatment of abnormal human development. For instance, screening drugs by testing them on cultured human embryonic stem cells could help reduce the risk of drug-related birth defects.

Embryonic Stem Cells Could Treat Disease

The ability to grow human tissue of all kinds opens the door to treating a range of cell-based diseases and to growing medically important tissues that can be used for transplantation purposes. For example, diseases like juvenile onset diabetes mellitus and Parkinson's disease occur because of defects in one of just a few cells types. Replacing faulty cells with healthy ones offers hope of lifelong treatment. Similarly, failing hearts and other organs, in theory, could be shored up by injecting healthy cells to replace damaged or diseased cells.

Adult Stem Cells Are Limited

There are several approaches now in human clinical trials that utilize mature stem cells (such as blood-forming cells, neuron-forming cells and cartilage-forming cells). However, because adult cells are already specialized, their potential to regenerate damaged tissue is very limited: skin cells will only become skin and cartilage cells will only become cartilage. Adults do not have stem cells in many vital organs, so when those tissues are damaged, scar tissue develops. Only embryonic stem cells, which have the capacity to become any kind of human tissue, have the potential to repair vital organs.

Pluripotent stem cells represent hope for millions of Americans.

Another limitation of adult stem cells is their inability to proliferate in culture. Unlike embryonic stem cells, which have a capacity to reproduce indefinitely in the laboratory, adult stem cells are difficult to grow in the lab and their potential to reproduce diminishes with age. Therefore, obtaining clinically significant amounts of adult stem cells may prove to be difficult.

Studies of adult stem cells are important and will provide valuable insights into the use of stem cell in transplantation procedures. However, only through exploration of all types of stem cell research will scientists find the most efficient and effective ways to treat diseases.

Scientists Need the Opportunity to Research

Pluripotent stem cells represent hope for millions of Americans. They have the potential to treat or cure a myriad of diseases, including Parkinson's, Alzheimer's, diabetes, heart disease, stroke, spinal cord injuries and burns.

This extraordinary research is still in its infancy and practical application will only be possible with additional study. Scientists need to understand what leads cells to specialization in order to direct cells to become particular types of tissue. For example, islet cells control insulin production in the pancreas, which is disrupted in people with diabetes. If an individual with diabetes is to be cured, the stem cells used for treatment must develop into new insulin-producing islet cells, not heart tissue or other cells. Research is required to determine how to control the differentiation of stem cells so they will be therapeutically effective. Research is also necessary to study the potential of immune rejection of the cells, and how to overcome that problem.

2

The Potential of Embryonic Stem Cell Therapy Is Exaggerated

Mary L. Davenport

Mary L. Davenport is a board member of the American Association of Pro Life Obstetricians and Gynecologists. She is also the medical correspondent for AmericanThinker.com, and her columns concerning embryonic stem cell research and other bioethical questions regularly appear on this Web site.

Stem cells have been at the center of a bioethical debate since the first embryonic stem cells were isolated in 1998. In the years since, claims of the curative potential of embryonic stem cells have been greatly exaggerated to proliferate interest and funding in this field of research. Adult stem cells have been ignored, even though these have shown, through numerous studies, the greatest therapeutic potential. In addition to the increased potential of adult stem cells, there is no danger that research companies will patent the resulting product; thus their use will prevent therapeutic stem cell research from becoming a corporate, money-making venture.

Scientists know that claims of imminent cures of disease using embryonic stem cells are junk science, whereas progress in adult stem cell research has been nothing short of spectacular. It is unfortunate that the mainstream media have exaggerated the prospects for embryonic stem cell research while ignoring the real results achieved with adult stem cells.

Mary L. Davenport, "The Truth about Stem Cell Research," *American Thinker*, September 9, 2004. Reproduced by permission.

Ron Reagan [son of President Ronald Reagan] presented a pathetic spectacle at the [2004] Democratic convention when he imagined a scenario in the next decade in which a doctor could 'take a few skin cells from your arm,' place the nucleus in a donor egg, zap it with electrical stimulation, culture the cells, and presto 'you're cured.' But no reputable researcher believes that embryonic stem cells show any promise in the near future of being clinically useful in humans, and success with animals has been minimal. In fact, recent discoveries that some adult stem cells can be turned into any cell type in the body may make discussion of embryonic stem cell therapies moot.

The Potential of Adult Stem Cells Is Obvious

The fact that adult stem cells have already produced remarkable cures, whereas embryonic stem cells have failed in this regard, should not come as a great surprise to anyone with a background in high school biology. When an embryo is created by the union of the sperm and egg, the cells begin to divide, creating embryonic stem cells from which all future tissues and organs are derived. Within days, the embryonic cells differentiate into three cell layers—ectoderm, mesoderm and endoderm. Cells in these layers continue to differentiate into tissues and organs. As the embryo matures into a fetus, child, and adult, some undifferentiated cells of the three types remain in various tissues such as bone marrow, fat, skin and olfactory tissue.

These adult stem cells are multipotent: they have the ability to turn into a variety of types of tissues. Successful stem cell therapies cause the DNA in the adult stem cells to further differentiate into more specific types of cells. There is no point in getting the adult stem cell to turn into a less differentiated type of cell, or using the more primitive embryonic stem cells. This would be going backward, in the opposite direction of providing a clinically useful therapy.

Embryonic Stem Cell Therapies Create Numerous Complications

Difficulties abound with proposed embryonic stem cell therapies. The growth of the more primitive embryonic stem cells is more difficult to control and leads to tumor formation. Additionally, the use of embryonic tissue foreign to the patient can potentially lead to problems with immune rejection of tissue, a problem not encountered in using a patient's own adult stem cells. And as Ron Reagan stated, embryonic stem cell therapy is dependent on cloning a 'donor egg,' which is actually a fertilized egg, or early embryo. There would be tremendous logistical difficulty in securing sufficient 'donor eggs' to create useful embryonic stem cell therapies for all the proposed recipients. Most embryos in fertility clinics are slated for use in fertility therapies, and only a tiny percentage are donated for research. In contrast, new sources of adult stem cells are continuously being discovered.

> *Significant scientific problems with embryonic cell research have become more apparent [since 2001], and no useful therapies in humans have emerged.*

Despite the widespread impression created by some politicians and pundits, the controversial decision by President [George W.] Bush in August, 2001 did not ban embryonic stem cell research. It merely limited government funding in the US to the 72 embryonic stem cell lines already in existence. Embryos can be destroyed in the process of extracting stem cells. The limitation was put on government sponsoring of research that involved further destruction of embryos. Unregulated embryonic stem cell research continues outside the US, and inside the US with private funding.

Significant scientific problems with embryonic cell research have become more apparent [since 2001], and no useful therapies in humans have emerged. An experiment showed that the use of embryonic cells in mice with Parkinson's led to brain tumors in 20% of the subjects. In another experiment in diabetic mice, embryonic stem cells were successfully converted to insulin-producing cells in the pancreas, but all the subjects died. This contrasts with the full cure of diabetes in mice using transplanted adult stem cells.

Success with Adult Stem Cells Is Progressing Quickly

Advances in adult stem cell research since Bush's 2001 decision have been nothing short of awesome. At a [2004] Senate hearing on cutting-edge adult stem cell research, two young women, victims of horrific automobile accidents causing spinal cord paralysis, actually walked into the hearing room. They described their dramatic improvement after spinal cord paralysis. They were treated in Portugal by transplantation of their own stem cells, taken from olfactory tissue that has the ability to form new nerve cells.

It would be tragic if political considerations and greed diverted funding away from fruitful lines of research utilizing adult stem cells.

In Germany, a cancer victim whose jaw had been removed re-grew bone tissue utilizing adult stem-cells from his own bone marrow, and was able to eat a bratwurst sandwich for the first time in nine years. Patients with Parkinson's disease have reported significant improvement, some even regaining their sense of taste and smell, with injections of GDNF, an adult stem cell related therapy. . . . Do No Harm, the web site

19

of a coalition of American scientists for ethical research, is replete with dozens more successful examples of cures from adult stem cell research. . . .

The Case Against Private Funding

The private sector has refused to invest in [embryonic stem cell] research because it is unlikely to provide useful products any time soon. Jim Kelly, a Colorado stem-cell activist who is a paraplegic, agrees with private venture capitalists and says, 'We have to use our limited resources efficiently. Money spent on embryonic stem cell research and human cloning is money that cannot be spent on (investigating) adult stem cells.' . . .

Yet another reason has emerged why there is incessant pressure for embryonic stem cell research, despite mounting evidence of its inferiority to adult stem cell research, in testimony before a Senate Committee on July 14, 2004. After discussing the cases of the two paralyzed young women who were now walking after adult stem cell treatment in Portugal, Dr. Jean Peduzzi-Nelson pointed out that an embryonic stem cell product could become patentable and potentially yield enormous profits. But an adult stem cell therapy, in which the patient's own cells were used, could not produce a patentable procedure or product according to current laws.

It would be tragic if political considerations and greed diverted funding away from fruitful lines of research utilizing adult stem cells, which show promise in producing the cures sought by so many desperate patients.

3

Human Embryonic Stem Cell Research Is Immoral

Scott Klusendorf

Scott Klusendorf is the president of the Life Training Institute, an organization dedicated to educating the public about the pro life cause and teaching individuals with a pro life stance how to justify their beliefs. In his writing, Klusendorf has addressed issues such as embryonic stem cell research and abortion.

Embryonic stem cell research necessitates the killing of a human embryo in order to harvest its stem cells. Even though defenders of stem cell research claim that these cells may be the key to helping others who suffer from various disorders, destroying embryos to obtain stem cells is morally wrong. Embryos are human beings, and no matter what good may come of embryo research, there is no justification for murdering a human in its earliest developmental stage in the name of medical therapy.

When advocates of embryonic stem cell research say that we have a moral obligation to save lives and promote cures, what they really mean is that human embryos should be cloned and killed for medical research. But you would never know it listening to their rhetoric.

Now I'm all for saving lives. I'm also for stem cell research. But I'm opposed to one kind of stem cell research that requires killing defenseless human beings so that others may (allegedly) benefit. That's immoral.

Embryos Are Humans with Stem Cells

Stem cells are fast growing, unspecialized cells that can reproduce themselves and grow new organs for the body. All 210 different types of human tissue originate from these primitive cells. Because they have the potential to grow into almost any kind of tissue including nerves, bones, and muscle, scientists believe that the introduction of healthy stem cells into a patient may restore lost function to damaged organs, especially the brain. Human embryos have an abundant supply of stem cells which scientists are eager to harvest in hopes of treating Parkinson's disease, Alzheimer's disease, and other illnesses. There's only one problem: You must kill the embryo to get its stem cells.

Advocates of embryonic stem cell research often reply that the embryos in question are not human organisms, but stem cells with the potential to become human beings. This is an unabashed lie. Embryos don't come from stem cells; they are living human beings that *have* stem cells. And extracting these cells is lethal for the tiny human subject.

Cloning Creates a Living Human Embryo

Closely related to embryonic stem cell research is the cloning technique known as Somatic Cell Nuclear Transfer, which involves creating a human embryo that is a genetic clone of the patient and then killing that embryo so we can harvest its stem cells. This virtually guarantees that the patient's body will not reject the transplanted cells. It also reduces human life to a commodity: Embryos are created for the express purpose of destroying them for medical research.

Somatic Cell Nuclear Transfer is a three-step process. First, an unfertilized egg is taken from a woman and its nucleus is removed. Next, genetic material (DNA) from the patient is placed inside the vacated egg. Chemicals are then added and a spark of electricity jolts the cell into dividing and growing into a cloned human embryo, which is later destroyed for its stem cells. [In 1996], this same technique gave us "Dolly," the first cloned sheep. . . .

Despite claims to the contrary, embryonic stem cell research is not morally complex.

Fearing public backlash, advocates of embryo stem cell research are trying to legalize cloning on the sly. First, they told us to distinguish "reproductive cloning," which everyone allegedly condemned, from "therapeutic cloning," which everyone knew could save lives. But the distinction is totally misleading because all cloning is reproductive. So-called "reproductive" cloning means allowing the cloned human to be born alive. "Therapeutic" cloning means creating him for research, but killing him before birth. In either case, the act of cloning is exactly the same and results in a living human embryo. Remember: A cloned human being is created when the nucleus is removed from a human egg and replaced with genetic material from a donor. Once this occurs, the act of cloning is complete. After that, the only question is how we will *treat* the cloned human being—kill him for research or allow him to grow and develop. . . .

Embryos Are Humans

Despite claims to the contrary, embryonic stem cell research is not morally complex. It comes down to just one question: Are the embryos in question members of the human family? If so, killing them to benefit others is a serious moral wrong. It treats the distinct human being, with his or her own inherent moral worth, as nothing more than a disposable instrument. Conversely, if embryos are not human, killing them to extract stem cells requires no more justification than pulling a tooth. My friend Frank Beckwith sums up the crux of the debate this way: "If I have a bad eye and you have a good one, can I forcibly take your good eye to make my bad one better?" Reply: Not if the donor is human. Hence, the ethical debate comes down to, What is the embryo—a human being or something else?

The facts of science make clear that from the earliest stages of development, embryos (whether produced through normal reproduction or cloning) are distinct, living, and whole human beings. True, they have yet to grow and mature, but they are whole human beings nonetheless. Leading embryology textbooks affirm this. . . .

The difference in kind between each of our cells and a human embryo is clear: An individual cell's functions are subordinated to the survival of the larger organism of which it is merely a part. The human embryo, however, is already a whole human entity. . . .

All Human Life Is Valuable

Some advocates of embryo stem cell research concede that zygotes (early embryos) are biologically human but deny that they are complex or developed enough to qualify as valuable human beings with a right to life. The argument goes that humans have value not in virtue of the kind of thing they are (members of a natural kind or species), but only because of an acquired property, usually, the immediate capacity for self-awareness. Zygotes and embryos do not have this immediate capacity and therefore fail to qualify as subjects of rights. "A goldfish resembles a human being more than an embryo does," writes journalist Michael Kinsley. "An embryo feels nothing, thinks nothing, cannot suffer, is not aware of its own existence." Go ahead and use it for research. Only blind faith can say that you shouldn't.

There are at least two problems that underscore the arbitrary and counterintuitive nature of Kinsley's claim. First, the self-awareness argument proves too much. Newborns are not aware of their own existence until several months after birth, so what's wrong with infanticide? As [medical ethicist] Peter Singer points out in *Practical Ethics*, if self-awareness makes one valuable, and newborns like fetuses lack that property, it follows that fetus and newborn are both disqualified. You can't draw an arbitrary line at birth and spare the newborn. Second, if humans have value only because of some acquired property like self-awareness or sentience and not in virtue of the kind of thing they are, then it follows that since these acquired properties come in varying degrees, basic human rights come in varying degrees. Does Kinsley really want to say that those with more self-awareness are more human (and more valuable) than those with less? This relegates the proposition that all men are created equal to the ash heap of history. Philosophically, it's far more reasonable to argue that although humans differ immensely with respect to talents, accomplishments, and degrees of development, they are nonetheless equal because they share a common human nature that comes to be when they come to be—either at conception or the completion of a cloning process.

Regrettably, moral concerns with embryo stem cell research are often dismissed . . . as anti-science and anti-progress.

In reply, some argue that destructive embryo research is justified because at least one source for human embryos, fertility clinics, have large numbers of "spare" embryos that are going to die anyway. Rather than discarding them, the argument goes, we should harvest their stem cells to treat disease in others. This is specious reasoning. One could, with equal validity, suggest that we allow research on six-month fetuses scheduled for partial-birth abortions. The fact is that we all die sometime. Do those of us who are going to die later have the right to kill (and exploit) those who will die sooner? Even if an individual's death is imminent, we still do not have a license to use him for lethal experiments. We cannot, for example, conduct experiments upon death-row prisoners or harvest their organs without their consent. Nor can we extract body parts from mortally wounded soldiers while they are dying on the battlefield.

Regrettably, moral concerns with embryo stem cell research are often dismissed (rather than refuted) as anti-science and anti-progress, much like the persecution of Galileo. "Our conviction about what is natural or right should not inhibit the role of science in discovering the truth," Tony Blair told critics of Britain's plan to clone human embryos for research. "[We will] not stand by as successful British science once more ends ups being manufactured abroad." Echoing these same sentiments, U.S. Senator Orin Hatch remarked, "It would be terrible to say because of an ethical concept, we can't do anything for patients." Ron Reagan, son of the late pro-life President [Ronald Reagan], told the [2004] Democratic National Convention that, "Many opponents to the research are well-meaning and sincere, but their beliefs are just that—an article of faith. . . . The theology of a few should not be allowed to forestall the health and well-being of many."

However, if Blair, Hatch, and Reagan are correct that scientific progress trumps morality, one can hardly condemn Hitler for grisly medical experiments on Jews. Nor can one criticize the Tuskegee experiments of the 1920s in which black men suffering from syphilis were promised treatment, only to have it denied so scientists could study the disease.

Ramesh Ponnuru writes that pro-cloning polemics frequently frame the debate in terms that obscure the point at issue. "A cloning ban is said to be an attempt to ban research, its supporters are said to fear knowledge, and it is opposed on that basis. It is, of course, true that a ban would bar certain types of research and could prevent certain knowledge from being discovered—but because the research to get the knowledge involves homicide, not because it is research."

Not All Stem Cell Research Is Immoral

Finally, not only is embryonic stem cell research immoral, it may be unnecessary. Numerous peer-reviewed studies indicate that adult stem cells are more effective at treating disease than previously thought. Unlike embryo stem cell research, we can extract these adult cells without harming the donor. Critics of the pro-life view, like the late actor Christopher Reeve, insist that these adult cells won't work. However, the evidence suggests just the opposite. . . .

Stem cells drawn from adults have already yielded some striking achievements, and they do not require the killing of the human being from whom they are drawn. The extraction of stem cells from human embryos does, however, result in the destruction of defenseless human beings. Therefore, it is morally wrong. There's nothing complex about it.

4

Human Embryonic Stem Cell Research Is Not Immoral

Michael Kinsley

Michael Kinsley is the editorial and opinions editor for the Los Angeles Times *and the founder of the online magazine* Slate. *Previously he has served as editor for numerous publications including* Slate, The New Republic, Harper's, *and the* Washington Monthly. *In these publications and others he has written extensively on both the stem cell research debate and the pro-life lobby.*

Fertility clinics across the United States continually create and store embryos for couples who hope to have children through the aid of in vitro fertilization. In order to ensure pregnancy, a large number of eggs are fertilized, creating a surplus of embryos. Often these extra embryos are destroyed. Still, many pro-life organizations herald in vitro fertilization as a miracle technology providing an opportunity for individuals to become pregnant who would otherwise be unable. Ironically, though, these same organizations also stridently oppose embryonic stem cell research due to the number of embryos killed. Yet it should be obvious that far more embryos are destroyed at fertility clinics than through stem cell experimentation. If this conflict in morality cannot be squared, then it is insincere to claim that stem cell research is an immoral practice.

Michael Kinsley, "False Dilemma on Stem Cells," *Washington Post*, July 7, 2006. Reproduced by permission of the author.

The issue of stem cell research . . . is often described as a moral dilemma, but it simply is not. Or at least it is not the moral dilemma often used in media shorthand: the rights of the unborn vs. the needs of people suffering from diseases that embryonic stem cells might cure. As one of those people myself (I have Parkinson's), I am not an objective analyst of what the U.S. government's continuing near-ban on stem cell research is costing our society and the world. Naturally, I think it's costing too much. No other potential therapy—including adult stem cells—is nearly as promising for my ailment and others. Evaluate that as you wish.

Against this, you have the fact that embryonic stem cells are extracted from human embryos, killing the latter in the process. If you believe that embryos a few days after conception have the same human rights as you or me, killing innocent embryos is obviously intolerable. But do opponents of stem cell research really believe that? Stem cell research tests that belief, and sharpens the basic right-to-life question, in a way abortion never has.

Fertility Clinics as the Source of Embryos

Here's why. Stem cells used in medical research generally come from fertility clinics, which produce more embryos than they can use. This isn't an accident—it is essential to their mission of helping people have babies. Often these are "test tube babies": the product of an egg fertilized in the lab and then implanted in a womb to develop until birth. Controversy about test-tube babies has all but disappeared. Vague science-fiction alarms have been crushed by the practical evidence, and potential political backlash, of grateful, happy parents.

In any particular case, fertility clinics try to produce more embryos than they intend to implant. Then—like the Yale admissions office (only more accurately)—they pick and choose among the candidates, looking for qualities that make for a better human being. If you don't get into Yale, you have the choice of attending a different college. If the fertility clinic rejects you, you get flushed away—or maybe frozen until the day you can be discarded without controversy.

And fate isn't much kinder to the embryos that make this first cut. Usually several of them are implanted in the hope that one will survive. Or, to put it another way, in the hope that all but one will not survive. And fertility doctors do their ruthless best to make these hopes come true.

In short, if embryos are human beings with full human rights, fertility clinics are death camps—with a side order of cold-blooded eugenics. No one who truly believes in the humanity of embryos could possibly think otherwise.

Fertility Clinics Destroy More Embryos than Stem Cell Research

And, by the way, when it comes to respecting the human dignity of microscopic embryos, nature—or God—is as cavalier as the most godless fertility clinic. The casual creation and destruction of embryos in normal human reproduction is one reason some people, including me, find it hard to make the necessary leap of faith to believe that an embryo and, say, Nelson Mandela are equal in the eyes of God.

Moral sincerity is not impressive it if depends on willful ignorance and indifference to logic.

Proponents of stem cell research like to emphasize that it doesn't cost the life of a single embryo. The embryos killed to extract their stem cells were doomed already. But this argument gives too much ground, and misses the point. If embryos are human beings, it's not okay to kill them for their stem cells just because you were going to kill them, or knowingly let them die, anyway. The better point—the killer point, if you'll pardon the expression—is that if embryos are human beings, the routine practices of fertility clinics are far worse—

both in numbers and in criminal intent—than stem cell research. And yet, no one objects, or objects very loudly. President Bush actually praised the work of fertility clinics in his first speech announcing restrictions on stem cells.

Even strong believers in abortion rights (I'm one) ought to acknowledge and respect the moral sincerity of many right-to-lifers. I cannot share, or even fathom, their conviction that a microscopic dot—as oblivious as a rock, more primitive than a worm—has the same human rights as anyone reading this article. I don't have their problem with the question of when human life begins. (When did "human" life begin during evolution? Obviously, there is no magic point. But that doesn't prevent us from claiming humanity for ourselves and denying it to the embryo-like entities we evolved from.) Nevertheless, abortion opponents deserve respect for more than just their right to hold and express an opinion we disagree with. Excluding, of course, the small minority who believe that their righteousness puts them above the law, sincere right-to-lifers deserve respect as that rarity in modern American politics: a strong interest group defending the interest of someone other than themselves.

Time to Reconsider the Pro-Life Stance on Stem Cell Research

Or so I always thought—until the arrival of stem cells. Moral sincerity is not impressive if it depends on willful ignorance and indifference to logic. Not every opponent of stem cell research deserves to have his or her debater's license taken away. There are a few, no doubt, who are as horrified by fertility clinics as they are by stem cell research, and a subset of this subset may even be doing something about it. But these people, if they exist, are not a political force strong enough to stop a juggernaut of medical progress that so many other people are desperate to encourage. The vast majority of people who oppose stem cell research either haven't thought it through, or have thought it through and don't care.

I wish they would think again.

5

An Embryo Should Be Regarded as a Human Being

Patrick Lee and Robert P. George

Patrick Lee is a professor of bioethics at Franciscan University of Steubenville, Ohio. Robert P. George is a member of President George W. Bush's Council on Bioethics, and the McCormick Professor of Jurisprudence and director of the James Madison Program in American Ideals and Institutions at Princeton University. They have collaborated on many articles concerning embryonic stem cell research, abortion, and the nature of human life.

Some proponents of stem cell research argue that an embryo is not human until it is 14 days old, and that the humanity of the embryo is not assured until its implantation in the mother's womb. However, research has shown that from the time of fertilization, all of the cells in an embryo work collectively to achieve higher development, proving conclusively that an embryo is a purposeful human life from the time it is conceived. Implantation in no way changes the nature of the embryo. Similarly, pre-implantation occurrences such as twinning and fusion, in which one embryo splits to become two or two embryos join to become one, do not disprove the humanness of the embryo because these processes are part of the complex development stages that still result in life.

In the debate about the moral standing of human embryos, some defenders of embryo-destructive research have claimed that human embryos are not human beings until implantation (i.e., when the embryo attaches to the uterus, approximately six days after fertilization), and others have claimed that they are not human beings until gastrulation (i.e., when the possibility of twinning no longer exists and the primitive neural streak first appears, approximately 14 days after fertilization). These claims have been repeated by policymakers, scientists, and bioethicists alike, yet they fly in the face of the embryological evidence. Seeing why will put the embryo research debate on a more solid biological footing.

Life Does Not Begin with Implantation

Over the past few years, Utah Senator Orrin Hatch has pushed aggressively for federal funding of embryo-destructive research. When it comes to abortion, Senator Hatch votes consistently pro-life; he believes we have a moral obligation to protect developing human beings. But he also believes that embryos produced outside of a woman's body, whether by cloning or in vitro fertilization, are not human beings unless or until they are implanted in a uterus. "At the core of my support for regenerative medicine research," he declared in 2002, "is my belief that human life requires and begins in a mother's nurturing womb."

More recently, William Neaves, president of the Stowers Institute for Medical Research in Kansas City, has similarly claimed in public hearings that the embryo does not become a human being until implantation. According to Neaves, not until the embryo receives external, maternal signals at implantation is it able to establish the basic body plan of the human, and only then does it become a self-directing human organism. According to Neaves, these signaling factors somehow transform what was hitherto a mere bundle of cells into a unitary organism.

In reply to Hatch, Neaves, and others who make this argument, the first point to notice is that the standard embryology texts locate the beginning of the human individual at fertilization, not at implantation. See, for example, William J. Larsen, *Human Embryology*, 3rd ed. (2001); Keith Moore and T.V.N. Persaud, *The Developing Human, Clinically Oriented Embryology*, 7th ed. (2003); and Ronan O'Rahilly and Fabiola Mueller, *Human Embryology and Teratology*, 3rd ed. (2000). Most people who point to implantation as the beginning of an individual human life—Senator Hatch is a prime example—offer not the slightest bit of evidence to support their claim, relying instead on an alleged intuition. But since such intuitions can be matched by contrary intuitions, and since the alleged intuitions of Hatch and others contradict the evidence supplied by embryological science, they have no evidential weight whatsoever.

The Case Against Implantation

Neaves does offer an actual argument, but it is severely flawed. He claims that at implantation maternal signaling factors transform a bundle of cells into a human organism. But there is much dispute about whether any such maternal signaling actually occurs. As [biologist] Hans-Werner Denker observes, it was once assumed that in mammals, in contrast to amphibians and birds, polarity in the early embryo depends upon some external signal, since no clear indications of bilateral symmetry had been found in oocytes, zygotes, or early blastocysts. But this view has been revised in light of emerging evidence: "[I]ndications have been found that in mammals the axis of bilateral symmetry is indeed determined (although at first in a labile way) by sperm penetration, as in amphibians. Bilateral symmetry can already be detected in the early blastocyst and is not dependent on implantation."

Denker refers specifically to the work of Magdalena Zernicka-Goetz and her colleagues at Cambridge and that of

R. L. Gardner at Oxford, which shows that polarity exists even at the two-cell stage. Davor Solter and Takashi Hiiragi of the Max Planck Institute for Immunobiology in Freiburg dispute these results, arguing that in the early embryo (prior to compaction and differentiation into inner cell mass and trophoblast) external factors determine the fate of each cell, rather than an internal polarity. As Gretchen Vogel reported in 2005 in *Science* magazine, embryologists are "polarized over early cell fate determination." It is no longer taken as certain that the bilateral polarity of the embryo does not occur in the very first cleavages.

Moreover—and more importantly—even if it *is* the case that polarity does not emerge until a maternal signal is received at implantation, that would *not* provide any evidence at all that such a signal transformed a bundle of cells into a unitary, multicellular human organism. Rather, just as the lungs begin to breathe at birth only in response to certain external stimuli, so it would make sense that differentiation into the rudiments of the distinct body parts (basic bilateral polarity) would begin only in response to some external stimuli. And this is exactly how such signals speculated to occur (perhaps) in mammalian embryos are interpreted by the embryology texts that mention them. Thus, Neaves not only treats uncertain data as definitive, but—more to the point—his claim fails to hold up even if, for the sake of argument, one grants his assumptions.

Purposeful Development from Day 1 to Day 6

The last point in reply to the claim that the human being is not generated until implantation is the most important one: there is complex and coordinated development from day 1 to day 6, much of it plainly oriented to preparing the embryo for the implantation process, as well as for processes that will occur only after that. The proposition that the human organism does not come to be until implantation (day 6) offers no explanation for this regular and ordered development.

Clearly, these activities—compaction, cavitation, and implantation itself—are organized processes performed by the embryo as an organismal whole.

On day 3 or 4 *compaction* occurs, which is the process in which the cells change their shapes and align themselves closely together. And compaction is the first step toward *cavitation*—the process (at day 4) in which an inner cavity is formed within the embryo and the embryo differentiates itself into the inner cell mass (which will later develop into the body of the mature organism) and the trophoblast (which will later develop into the placenta, a temporary organ of the embryo, equivalent to other temporary parts of the body, like baby teeth). On day 5 or 6, as the embryo enters the uterus, it "hatches" from the zona pellucida—the membrane enveloping the ovum that the sperm had to penetrate for fertilization to occur—preparing to begin implantation. At the same time, the trophoblast cells secrete an enzyme which erodes the epithelial lining of the uterus and creates an implantation site for the embryo.

In addition, the trophoblast itself becomes differentiated (about day 3 or 4) into various levels (cytotrophoblast and syncytiotrophoblast) in preparation for developing the vital contacts with the mother's blood system (the embryo will circulate its own blood but will exchange oxygen and wastes with the mother's blood, first through connecting microvilli, and eventually through the umbilical cord, developed from the trophoblast). Around the same time, the trophoblast produces immunosuppressive factors signaling the mother's system to accept the embryo rather than attack it as a foreign substance. In order for the embryo as a whole to survive, this complex series of activities must occur in a timely, ordered sequence and with predictable regularity. Clearly, these activities—compaction, cavitation, and implantation itself—are organized processes performed by the embryo as an organismal whole.

The actions of the embryo from day 1 to day 6 are clearly part of a unitary development toward human maturation.

The test of whether a group of cells constitutes a single organism is whether they form a stable body and function as parts of a whole, self-developing, adaptive unit. Compaction, cavitation, the changes occurring earlier to facilitate these activities, and implantation—all of these activities are clear cases of the cells acting in a coordinated manner for the sake of a self-developing and adaptive whole. In other words, such activities are ordered to the survival and maturation of the whole, existing embryo. This fact shows that the unity of the blastomeres (the cells of the early embryo) is *substantial* rather than incidental; the blastomeres are integrated parts of a functional whole, not separate parts that lead to the creation of a whole. This is compelling evidence that what exists from day 1 to day 6 is not a mere aggregate of cells but a multi-cellular organism.

The Beginning of Development Is Essential to Later Development

Of course, one might object that even if there is an organism from day 1 to day 6, perhaps it is not the same as the organism after day 6. Perhaps implantation and its concomitant events produce a substantial change, the generation of a new organism. In reality, however, the direction of the growth between day 1 and day 6, on the one hand, and from day 6 onward, on the other hand, is the same. That is, the sequence of steps in the embryo from day 1 to day 6 is necessary and preparatory for what occurs afterward, and is a unitary trajectory of development. It is unlike, for example, the separate sequences of events undergone by the sperm and the ovum, respectively, before fertilization. Gametes (sperm and ovum) are oriented to joining with each other, actions that are performed not by them as a single unit, but by the maternal and paternal organisms (i.e., the mother and father). The sperm and the ovum (prior to fusing) are distinct biological parts of the distinct parent organisms (even though in coitus a type of organic union is effected between the male and female organisms). By contrast, the human embryo's cells (from day 1 onward) form a stable body and work together to produce a single direction of growth, which is toward the maturation of the human organism.

The actions of the embryo from day 1 to day 6 are clearly part of a unitary development toward human maturation. None of the events occurring in the embryo could reasonably be interpreted as creating a new and distinct direction. Implantation does not change the *nature* (kind of being) of the embryo; it is an event in the unfolding life of a whole human organism, not the initiation of an entirely new organism.

Twinning and Fusion Do Not Contradict Individuality

Another attempt to locate the beginning of the human being after fertilization is based on the rare phenomenon of monozygotic twinning and the even rarer phenomenon of fusion. Monozygotic twinning occurs when embryonic division results in two whole embryos. Apparently, fusion can also occur in humans: that is, two embryos can fuse to become one embryo. Such twinning and fusion are possible up to approximately day 14, with the appearance of the primitive streak, the visible precursor of the spinal cord and brain. Some argue that the possibility of twinning or fusion shows that prior to day 14 the embryo is not an individual; the individual who is clearly present at more mature stages of development has not yet come to be. [Philosophy professor] Raymond Devettere expresses the argument clearly:

> If we say a zygote is one of us, then we are also saying that one of us can become two of us, and that two of us can become one of us. This makes no sense. The possibility of the zygotes' splitting or fusing suggests the zygote is not yet what we mean by one of us.

The puzzle, some seem to suppose, is that if we trace someone's life back to adolescence, then to infancy, then to fetal existence, and then back to the embryonic stage, it does not seem as though the individual's life traces back to fertilization. The tracing, in some cases, seems to stop at twinning or fusion.

But there is no puzzle here. Although twinning and fusion raise interesting questions about the details of early embryonic life, the argument that an individual life is not yet present is simply fallacious. Rather, in twinning, either the first embryo dies and gives rise to two others, or the first embryo continues to live and a second embryo is generated upon the splitting of the first one. We think the latter alternative is more likely, that twinning is (like induced cloning) a type of asexual reproduction in which the second embryo is reproduced asexually. For although monozygotic twinning *can* occur at the two-cell stage, most monozygotic twinning (at least two-thirds) occurs between days 5 and 9. In those cases, the growth trajectory of the original embryo continues, though the separation of some of the cells from the inner cell mass generates another embryo, with a distinct development trajectory. (If the splitting occurs after day 9, the embryos may share some of their permanent organs, resulting in conjoined twins, which are two distinct organisms that possess some degree of organic union.) The possibility of embryo fusion also poses no difficulty for the individuality of the embryo from day 1. If fusion in fact occurs, one embryo is absorbed into the system of another. . . .

Embryos Consistently Behave in a Deliberate and Complex Manner

Viewed biologically, the occurrence of monozygotic twinning and the possibility of fusion fail to show that in the first fourteen days the cells within the embryo constituted only an incidental mass. Just as the division of a single, whole flatworm into two whole flatworms does not show that prior to that division the flatworm was not a unitary individual, just so with the human embryo that twins. Parts of a flatworm have the potential to become a whole flatworm when isolated from the present whole of which they are part. Likewise, at the early stages of an embryo's development, the degree of cellular specialization has not progressed very far (even if the process of orderly cellular activity is underway from the beginning), which means the embryo's cells or groups of cells can become whole organisms if they are divided and have an appropriate environment after the division. But that does not show that prior to such an extrinsic division the embryo is a mere mass of cells rather than a single, complex, actively developing human organism.

We must not let the desire to use human embryos in research obscure our grasp of what those embryos truly are from day 1.

There is additional, decisive evidence for this point: if the individual cells within the embryo before twinning were each independent of the others, there would be no reason why each would not regularly develop on its own. But as we know, these allegedly independent, non-communicating cells actually function together to develop into a single, more mature member of the human species. This fact shows that interaction is taking place between the cells from the very beginning (even within the zona pellucida, before implantation), restraining them from individually developing as whole organisms and directing each of them to function as a part of a single, whole organism identical with the zygote. This means that prior to an extrinsic division of the embryo's cells resulting in the existence of a twin, these cells together constitute a single organism. And prior to the (even rarer) event of fusion, the twin embryos that fuse are distinct, whole organisms exhibiting active development.

Science has not solved every mystery of early human development. But human embryology has advanced sufficiently to enable us to dismiss certain fallacies about when a new human life comes to be. . . . We must not let the desire to use human embryos in research obscure our grasp of what those embryos truly are from day 1: namely, nascent members of the human species, worthy of that fundamental respect and protection that justice demands for every member of the human family.

6

Banning Stem Cell Research Violates Human Rights

David Holcberg and Alex Epstein

David Holcberg is a media specialist at the Ayn Rand Institute, an organization that seeks to promote rational self-interest, reason, and individual rights—elements of the life philosophy of author Ayn Rand. Alex Epstein is a junior fellow at the Ayn Rand Institute. Both Holcberg and Epstein have written on a variety of issues concerning the rights of American citizens.

In American society, all citizens are granted the right to pursue life and happiness. These rights ensure that people interact fairly and in freedom. Embryos, however, are only potential citizens and thus do not yet need or warrant the rights afforded by society. If embryos were granted the rights of participants, other members of society would be denied their rights. For example, scientists would be robbed of their right to engage in studies that could enhance human life. In addition, those future generations who might benefit from the work of these scientists would also suffer needlessly. For these reasons, it is essential that stem cell research must proceed unhindered.

It is widely known that embryonic stem cell research has the potential to revolutionize medicine and save millions of lives. Yet many U.S. senators, following the lead of President George [W.] Bush, are frantically working to defeat a measure [the Stem Cell Research Enhancement Act of 2005] that would

David Holcberg and Alex Epstein, "Commentary: Belief-based Opposition to Stem-Cell Research and Absurdity," *Medical Device Week*, August 9, 2005. Reproduced by permission.

expand federal financing of this research. Why are they and so many others opposing embryonic stem cell research—and doing so under the banner of being "pro-life"?

Embryos Are Only Potential Humans

The opponents of embryonic stem cell research claim that their position is rooted in "respect for human life." They say that the embryos destroyed in the process of extracting stem cells are human beings with a right to life.

But embryos used in embryonic stem cell research are manifestly not human beings—not in any rational sense of the term. These embryos are smaller than a grain of sand, and consist of at most a few hundred undifferentiated cells. They have no body or body parts. They do not see, hear, feel, or think. While they have the potential to become human beings—if implanted in a woman's uterus and brought to term—they are nowhere near actual human beings.

What, then, is the pro-lifers' reason for regarding these collections of cells as sacred and attributing rights to them? Religious dogma.

Rights Are Granted to Humans by Humans

The pro-lifers accept on faith the belief that rights are a divine creation: a gift from an unknowable supernatural being bestowed on embryos at conception (which many extend to embryos "conceived" in a beaker). The most prominent example of this view is the official doctrine of the Catholic church, which declares to its followers that an embryo "is to be respected and treated as a person from the moment of conception; and therefore from that same moment his rights as a person must be recognized."

But rights are not some supernatural construct, mystically granted by the will of God. They are this-worldly principles of proper political interaction rooted in man's rational nature. Rights recognize the fact that men can only live successfully and happily among one another if they are free from the initiation of force against them. Rights exist to protect and further human life. Rights enable individual men to think, act, produce and trade, live and love in freedom. The principle of rights is utterly inapplicable to tiny, pre-human clusters of cells that are incapable of such actions.

Granting Embryos Rights Will Have Devastating Consequences

In fact, to attribute rights to embryos is to call for the violation of actual rights. Since the purpose of rights is to enable individuals to secure their well-being, a crucial right, inherent in the right to liberty and property, is the right to do scientific research in pursuit of new medical treatments. To deprive scientists of the freedom to use clusters of cells to do such research is to violate their rights—as well as the rights of all who would contribute to, invest in, or benefit from this research.

In the name of the actual sanctity of human life and the inviolability of rights, embryonic stem cell research must be allowed to proceed unimpeded.

And to the extent that rights are violated in this way, we can expect deadly results. The political pressure against embryonic stem cell research is already discouraging many scientists and businessmen from investing their time and resources in its pursuit. If this research can lead, as scientists believe, to the ability to create new tissues and organs to replace damaged ones, any obstacles placed in its path will unnecessarily delay the discovery of new cures and treatments for diseases such as Parkinson's, Alzheimer's, osteoporosis and diabetes. Every day that this potentially life-saving research is delayed is another day that will go by before new treatments become available to ease the suffering and save the lives of countless individuals. And if the "pro-lifers" ever achieve the ban they seek on embryonic stem cell research, millions upon millions of human beings, living or yet to be born, might be deprived of healthier, happier and longer lives.

The enemies of embryonic stem cell research know this, but are unmoved. They are brazenly willing to force countless human beings to suffer and die for lack of treatments, so that clusters of cells remain untouched.

The Pro-Life Stance Is Contradictory

To call such a stance "pro-life" is beyond absurd. Their allegiance is not to human life or to human rights, but to their anti-life dogma.

If these enemies of human life wish to deprive themselves of the benefits of stem cell research, they should be free to do so and die faithful to the last. But any attempt to impose their religious dogma on the rest of the population is both evil and unconstitutional. While there are rational and valid arguments for opposing government involvement in scientific research as such, arguments that single out specific types of research on religious grounds should be dismissed without consideration. In the name of the actual sanctity of human life and the inviolability of rights, embryonic stem cell research must be allowed to proceed unimpeded. Our lives may depend on it.

7

Stem Cell Research Should Be Federally Funded

Sam Berger

Sam Berger is a research assistant at the Center for American Progress, a progressive think tank that seeks to influence public policy in order to make government more open and effective.

The 2006 state government elections proved that political supporters of stem cell research have the mandate of the American people. Both Republican and Democrat governors across the country have heeded the public's wishes and continued funding stem cell research even as President George W. Bush has placed further limits on national funding. With so much evidence of nationwide, bipartisan support for stem cell research, the White House needs to reconsider its restrictive and unpopular policy.

The tremendous support for embryonic stem cell research in the states should serve as a wake up call to the national government. In the true spirit of federalism, states have acted as laboratories of democracy, demonstrating in test after test the extensive support for the research among a broad swath of Americans.

Opponents of embryonic stem cell research have slowed efforts to support scientific advancements at the national level, but states are actively responding to the people's cries for cures. Although state efforts cannot replace federal funding, regulation, and research coordination, action on the part of states has helped to move the science forward while the national government lags behind public consensus. The national government should heed the example set in the states and modernize our stem cell policy to pursue life-saving cures and strengthen American competitiveness more aggressively.

Examples of State Support

State support for stem cell research was strong in the run-up to the 2006 election. Gov. John Baldacci (D-ME) announced a new initiative to increase biomedical research funding in Maine, both private and public, to $1 billion annually by 2010, explicitly mentioning increasing funding for stem cell research. Gov. Bill Richardson (D-NM) announced a plan to spend $10 million over three years on stem cell research, including building new research facilities for adult and embryonic stem cell research. And gubernatorial candidate Eliot Spitzer promised to spend $1 billion over 10 years on stem cell research if elected in New York.

These supporters of embryonic stem cell research were well rewarded in the 2006 elections. Research proponents were extremely successful in national races, and were even more successful at the state level. Govs. Baldacci and Richardson were both reelected after their calls for increased stem cell research funding. Gov. Jim Doyle (D-WI), who made support for the research a cornerstone of his first term and of his candidacy, handily won reelection. Gov. Spitzer (D-NY) was elected in New York, and governors who support the research were also elected in Massachusetts, Maryland, Illinois, and Kansas.

Support for embryonic stem cell research also stretched beyond traditionally liberal states. Research supporters Chet Culver, Ted Strickland, and Jennifer Granholm won governor's races in Iowa, Ohio, and Michigan respectively, with all three calling on their states to loosen onerous restrictions on the research. Also, the election of Gov. Charles Crist (R-FL), an embryonic stem cell proponent, as well as the reelection of Gov. Arnold Schwarzenegger (R-CA) and Gov. Jodi Rell (R-CT) demonstrated once again the bipartisan nature of the support for this work.

A less restrictive national policy is crucial to speeding the race towards life-saving cures.

Most notably, Missouri, which has long been considered a bellwether state for the nation, passed a constitutional amendment to protect embryonic stem cell research. The amendment will ensure that the science proceeds in the state, and that Missouri can continue its efforts to become a biomedical research hub.

Observing the success of the amendment, Gov. Kathleen Sebelius (D-KS) is considering a similarly worded amendment in her state in order to protect the research. Recent polling has shown that over 65 percent of Kansans support stem cell research, and almost 80 percent believed that "any stem cell research, therapies or cures that are permitted by federal law should be allowed in Kansas." This level of support is reflected in many other conservative states; a recent poll in Georgia showed that 67 percent of registered voters in Georgia support the research as well.

The Federal Government Should Follow Suit

Now the time has come for the federal government to follow suit, and fund research using newer stem cell lines. While states have been admirable in their support for embryonic stem cell research using new stem cell lines, a less restrictive national policy is crucial to speeding the race towards life-saving cures.

States have devoted a large amount of money to the research, but their funding is dwarfed by the federal government's resources. Through 2006, 90 percent of the funding for stem cell research had come from the federal government, but remains restricted to research using older stem cell lines. Worse yet, federally purchased labs and equipment cannot be used for research on stem cell lines that are ineligible for federal funding, forcing states to waste money separating state and federally funded equipment and staff, purchasing redundant equipment, and building new laboratories.

Separate state initiatives will also lead to a patchwork quilt of regulation, with different standards and practices slowing research and leading to redundancy. More expansive federal funding and regulation is needed to provide uniform standards and effective research coordination.

The national government would do well to heed the example set by the states on supporting embryonic stem cell research. Efforts in the states to adequately fund and protect the research have been met with tremendous support among diverse constituencies across the country. The laboratories of the states have been as effective demonstrating the public support for this research as scientific laboratories have been in proving its tremendous medical potential. In the recent election, the silent majority of stem cell supporters made their voice heard loud and clear. Congress and the president would do well to listen.

8

Embryonic Stem Cell Research Should Not Be Federally Funded

America

America is a national Catholic weekly magazine covering opinion, news, and book reviews. The print version of the magazine began in 1909.

Embryonic stem cell research is a divisive issue, and one that involves the destruction of a form of human life. Although stem cell research may lead to medical breakthroughs, there is no reason to compel those who object to embryonic research to help fund controversial therapies that conflict with their moral views. Instead, the federal government should support adult stem cell research because it does not involve the destruction of life and is therefore morally tolerable to most Americans.

The debate about stem cell research focuses on money and morality, on how to pay for this enterprise and how to guarantee that it is guided by ethical principles. In California [in November 2004], 60 percent of the voters dealt with the first of these concerns but not with the second. They passed Proposition 71, an initiative that authorizes the state to float a bond issue that will provide $3 billion over 10 years for one specific and controversial type of stem cell research: experimentation with stem cells harvested from human embryos about a week old.

The voters who supported Proposition 71 hope that embryonic stem cell research will eventually lead to nearly miraculous therapies. These cells are undifferentiated and have the potential of changing—morphing, as it is called—into the cells that build up tissues and organs in other parts of the body. Biomedical researchers speculate that it may one day be possible to infuse embryonic stem cells into the brain of a victim of Parkinson's disease or into the pancreas of a diabetic patient to effect a cure by replacing damaged cells.

It is important to note, however, that so far not even one cure has been effected using embryonic stem cells. Moreover, it is not certain that infusions of embryonic stem cells would be safe. They might also proliferate wildly and generate lethal tumors.

The Integrity of Embryos

The voters who rejected Proposition 71 did not do so because they were indifferent to the sufferings of disabled people. Some may have judged the bond issue plan too risky, but many appear to have been motivated by moral considerations. Embryonic stem cells are gathered for research purposes by a procedure that destroys the embryos. Some scientists may remark dismissively that these tiny embryos, regularly described as no bigger than a grain of sand, are no more than a cluster of cells. But other observers, including biologists, recognize the embryo as a human life at the very beginning of its existence. One need not be either a cytologist or a Christian to agree with the *Catechism of the Catholic Church* when it says that the human embryo should be respected and defended in its integrity.

Some advocates of embryonic stem cell research seem to conceal, or at least rarely mention, the presence of other sources from which stem cells may be derived without fatal consequences. They can be culled from adult tissue—from bone marrow, for example—without harming the donor.

Moreover, there are already on record instances of significant healings that have been achieved through adult stem cell therapy.

Embryonic stem cell research should not be subsidized by public funds.

To be sure, California may find itself too financially strapped to appropriate those billions for embryonic stem cell research. Whatever the outcome, the state's electorate has stepped up the momentum of a debate that is likely to grow more heated, because it is intertwined with intensely poignant problems of human suffering.

Find Less Destructive and Controversial Research

In this debate, however, there are some points on which all sides can agree. There is, to begin with, a general consensus that scientific research and the astonishing technology that it has made possible are great human endeavors that should be advanced, as long as their development is in accord with moral norms. All decent people will also agree that the compassionate care of the sick and disabled is an obligation shared by the whole human family.

There are, of course, differences in defining the precise ethical standards that should govern both biomedical research and the care of the sick. It is sometimes said that people who are not experts in these fields are not qualified to judge what is right or wrong. Ordinary citizens can properly point out that one need not know how to make nuclear weapons to know that hydrogen bombs should not be dropped on cities.

The debate over embryonic stem cell research cannot be fully resolved, because it is ignited by irreconcilable views of what reverence for life requires. It should be possible, however, to define the role of government in this contested area in a way that respects the moral convictions of all parties to the debate.

Embryonic stem cell research should not be subsidized by public funds. It is already well subsidized by private sources, and this will continue because of the commercial possibilities for pharmaceutical companies. On the other hand, federal and state monies should be used to support adult stem cell research. [In 2003] the National Institutes for Health allotted $191 million for adult stem cell studies. If this relatively tiny sum were greatly expanded, researchers might develop therapies that would be ethical, effective and safe. The Secretariat for Pro-Life Activities sponsored by the U.S. Catholic bishops has a neat slogan for this goal: "Let's Find Cures We Can All Live With."

9

No Form of Stem Cell Research Should Be Federally Funded

Ron Paul

Ron Paul is a member of the U.S. House of Representatives from Texas. He embraces libertarian politics, emphasizing limited constitutional government, low taxes, and free markets. He has also authored several books, including Challenge to Liberty; The Case for Gold; *and* A Republic, If You Can Keep It.

The controversy over federal funding of stem cell research is highly politicized and divides the American public along religious, moral, and ethical lines. Congress cannot be the arbiter of such a debate; only the states and individuals can decide whether this research can continue within their communities. Asking the federal government to weigh in on the issue would jeopardize personal liberty by imposing morality from above. In addition, federal funding may upset the natural progress of research by enticing researchers to pursue stem cell therapies at the expense of investigating other potentially worthwhile medical treatments. Therefore, the federal government should neither support nor condemn any form of stem cell research.

Medical and scientific ethics issues are in the news again, as Congress narrowly passed a bill [in May 2005] that funds controversial embryonic stem cell research. While I certainly sympathize with those who understandably hope such

Ron Paul, "Missing the Point: Federal Funding of Stem Cell Research," LewRock well.com, May 31, 2005. Reproduced by permission.

research will lead to cures for terrible diseases, I object to forcing taxpayers who believe harvesting embryos is immoral to pay for it.

Congressional Republicans, eager to appease pro-life voters while still appearing suitably compassionate, supported a second bill that provides nearly $80 million for umbilical cord stem cell research. But it's never compassionate to spend other people's money for political benefit.

Government Should Not Support Unpopular Research

The issue is not whether the federal government should fund one type of stem cell research or another. The issue is whether the federal government should fund stem cell research at all. Clearly there is no constitutional authority for Congress to do so, which means individual states and private citizens should decide whether to permit, ban, or fund it. Neither party in Washington can fathom that millions and millions of Americans simply don't want their tax dollars spent on government research of any kind. This viewpoint is never considered.

Rigid, centralized, government decision-making is indicative of an apathetic and immoral society.

Federal funding of medical research guarantees the politicization of decisions about what types of research for what diseases will be funded. Scarce tax resources are allocated according to who has the most effective lobby, rather than on the basis of need or even likely success. Federal funding also causes researchers to neglect potential treatments and cures that do not qualify for federal funds. Medical advancements often result from radical ideas and approaches that are scoffed at initially by the establishment. When scientists become dependent on government funds, however, they quickly learn not to rock the boat and stick to accepted areas of inquiry. Federal funds thus distort the natural market for scientific research.

Congress Cannot Be a Moral Arbiter

The debate over stem cell research involves profound moral, religious, and ethical questions—questions Congress is particularly ill equipped to resolve. The injustice of forcing taxpayers to fund research some find ethically abhorrent is patently obvious. When we insist on imposing one-size-fits-all social policies determined in Washington, we invariably make millions of Americans very angry. Again, the constitutional approach to resolving social issues involves local, decentralized decision-making. This approach is not perfect, but it is much better than pretending Congress possesses the magical wisdom to serve as the nation's moral arbiter. Decentralized decisions and privatized funding would eliminate much of the ill will between supporters and opponents of stem cell research.

Government cannot instill morality in the American people. On the contrary, rigid, centralized, government decision-making is indicative of an apathetic and immoral society. The greatest casualty of centralized government decision-making is personal liberty.

10

The Government Must Regulate Stem Cell Research

Bernadine P. Healy

Bernadine P. Healy is a medical doctor who served as the president of the American Red Cross from 1999 to 2001 and the director of the National Institutes of Health during the presidency of George H.W. Bush. Since 2002 she has served as a health editor for U.S. News & World Report.

In the Western world, America alone has no laws regarding human embryo research. Part of the reason why the United States lacks prescribed guidelines has to do with moral and religious disagreements over whether human embryos are people or merely collections of cells. America must face this and other difficult questions, however, before the science of embryo experimentation becomes unmanageable. Only by creating laws that apply justly to all experimenters can the public's confusion and concern over embryo research be tempered.

The United States is in the midst of a gold rush over human-embryo research. Not to be outdone by California's Proposition 71, which affirmed research cloning and committed $3 billion for stem-cell work, New Jersey became the second state to support embryo creation for research as part of its more modest stem-cell initiative. Now numerous other states, including Massachusetts, Maryland, and Wisconsin, are jumping in with proposals to similarly fund research cloning, also called somatic cell nuclear transfer, or SCNT. Compared with most other countries, the United States has become the Wild West, awash in private and public money looking toward human benefit and hefty economic returns.

America the Unregulated

This is happening against the backdrop of a resounding but nonbinding vote [in March 2005] by the United Nations calling for all governments to ban the cloning of human embryos for any purpose. This call echoes a raft of legislation by individual nations. A Swiss law that took effect earlier [in March] is typical of laws in most European countries: It bans embryo creation outright. That is, it forbids scientists from creating human research embryos by any means, including cloning, fertilizing eggs, or making chimeras—hybrid embryos of humans and animals. Scientists can work with spare embryos left over from in vitro fertilization [IVF], but that must be authorized by the state. Violators face hefty fines and jail time. Britain and Belgium allow embryo creation for research but don't make it easy. Britain has an independent embryo authority to scrutinize and monitor all projects and has issued only two cloning licenses since 2001.

The halo around stem-cell promise can easily obscure deep moral and religious issues surrounding many dimensions of this work.

What has made the United States such fertile ground for expanding embryo research is not its liberal laws but the lack of them. Congress has tried but failed to pass legislation largely because of irreconcilable metaphysical differences over when life begins. Both Presidents Bill Clinton and George W. Bush banned the National Institutes of Health [NIH] on ethical grounds from funding the creation of human research embryos, although their orders apply only to federally funded work. In 2001, Bush additionally narrowed NIH research to embryonic stem cells already harvested from spare IVF embryos. These restrictions triggered an outpouring of private and state funding, and the dramatic Proposition 71. Meanwhile, Bush pushed NIH funding of adult stem cells, which are not ethically challenged, and are proving, unexpectedly, to be almost as versatile as embryonic cells though not as plentiful. It's too early to choose a winner here, but the research largess from all sectors is unprecedented.

Avoiding or Obscuring Important Questions

Most Americans are for stem-cell research, but grasping critical differences between adult and embryonic cells, or the vocabulary of cloning, SCNT, and IVF, can be mind-boggling. It's easy to talk about the wonder of stem cells but harder to see the nuances of their creation. That has handicapped us in coming to a national consensus. Furthermore, the halo around stem-cell promise can easily obscure deep moral and religious issues surrounding many dimensions of this work.

A human embryo in its earliest ball-of-cells stage is still not the same as a lab rat. Creating such embryos to be research tools of commercial value tugs at the moral fiber of society and raises numerous ethical and social issues that are simply not being addressed by the silence of the law. How about women, the invisible research subjects here? South Korea made the first human embryonic cell lines from a clone [in 2004], using 242 human eggs to do so [a claim later proved to be fraudulent]. Many women faced the risk of daily hormone injections to artificially pump up their ovaries to the size of oranges filled with maturing eggs, which were then harvested for cloning. How can we assure that students in search of tuition, poor women in need of income, or junior lab workers wanting to support a research effort are not exploited?

A national effort to develop legally enforceable guidelines to oversee human-embryo research is urgently needed. And the rules must be clear, transparent to the public, and apply to all. The outcome might be one that allows for regulated embryo creation as in Britain or bans it for now as in most other nations. Doing nothing will keep stem-cell biology wealthy for a while, but science unregulated and mired in controversy will be damaging in the long run.

11

Therapeutic Cloning of Human Embryos Should Be Banned

Wesley J. Smith

Bioethics expert Wesley J. Smith is a senior fellow at the Discovery Institute, which promotes the principles of representative government, free markets, and individual liberty. Smith is also an attorney for the International Task Force on Euthanasia and Assisted Suicide and a special consultant for the Center for Bioethics and Culture. His books include Forced Exit: The Slippery Slope from Assisted Suicide to Legalized Murder *and* Culture of Death: The Assault on Medical Ethics in America.

Experimenting in the use of cloned embryonic stem cells to achieve miracle cures for debilitating illnesses is a dangerous avenue for science to pursue. Not only is such therapeutic cloning unproven, but also the number of human embryos required would be daunting and ethically questionable. For instance, current therapeutic cloning experiments involving animals succeed in a ratio of one out of one hundred attempts. If this is extrapolated to human treatments, the number of donor eggs required to succeed in curing the estimated 100 million needy patients would be staggering. Of course, such treatments might not be successful at all because no one can yet predict how stem cells will react when implanted in patients. For these reasons, the government should never consider removing the ban on funding embryonic stem cell research.

Polls show that most Americans want to ban all human cloning. President [George W.] Bush is eager to sign such a measure into law. The House has twice enacted a strong legal prohibition with wide, bipartisan votes. But cloning advocates have so far blocked passage of a ban in the Senate [the Brownback-Landrieu Human Cloning Prohibition Act] by asserting that "therapeutic cloning" might someday provide stem cell treatments for horrible illnesses such as Parkinson's and multiple sclerosis. (I believe the term "therapeutic cloning," is loaded and misleading. However, I use it here because the term is currently part of the popular lexicon.)

If it takes 100 or more tries to make a single human cloned embryonic stem cell line, therapeutic cloning is all but doomed as a viable future medical treatment.

An Exaggerated Example

According to the Biotechnology Industry Organization, the biotech industry's lobbying arm, here's how therapeutic cloning would work:

Suppose a middle-aged man suffers a serious heart attack while hiking in a remote part of a National Park. By the time he reaches the hospital, only a third of his heart is still working, and it is unlikely he will be able to return to his formerly active life. He provides scientists a small sample of skin cells. Technicians remove the genetic material from the cells and inject it into donated human eggs from which the chromosomes have been removed. These altered eggs [actually, cloned embryos] will yield stem cells that are able to form heart muscle cells. Since they are a perfect genetic match for the patient, these cells can be transplanted into his heart without causing his immune system to reject them. They grow and replace the cells lost during the heart attack, returning him to health and strength.

This scenario is typical of the hype that has pervaded discussions of therapeutic cloning over the last few years. But now, cold reality is setting in. Biotech researchers and cloning advocates are admitting difficulties in their professional journals, if not yet in the popular press, that make therapeutic cloning look more like a pipe dream than a realistic hope.

A High Rate of Failure

Consider a paper by Peter Mombaerts of Rockefeller University, "Therapeutic Cloning in the Mouse" . . . published by the National Academy of Sciences (NAS) [in 2003]. Mombaerts has been investigating therapeutic cloning techniques in mice. It has been tough going. Of these efforts, he sadly reports, "The efficiency, or perhaps better, the lack of efficiency thereof, is remarkably consistent." It takes about 100 tries to obtain one viable cloned mouse embryonic stem cell line.

Mombaerts notes that creating human cloned embryos using "nuclear transfer is unlikely to be much more efficient" than it is in mice, especially given that "the efficiency of nuclear transfer has not increased over the years in any of the mammalian species cloned." Nuclear transfer, more precisely somatic cell nuclear transfer (SCNT), is the same procedure used to create Dolly the sheep [the first cloned mammal]. The nucleus from an egg is removed and replaced with the nucleus from a clone donor's somatic cell, such as a skin cell. The modified egg is stimulated with an electric current. If the cloning "works," a cloned embryo is created that then develops just like a naturally created embryo.

Given the significant difficulties researchers have already had, deriving cloned embryonic stem cell lines is likely to be far less efficient in humans than it has been in mice (assuming that it can be accomplished at all).

This is big news and let's hope senators are paying attention. If they are, it should sink the rival to Brownback/ Landrieu, Orrin Hatch and Dianne Feinstein's cynically misnamed Human Cloning Ban and Stem Cell Research Protection Act of 2003, which would not outlaw human cloning at all but would explicitly legalize it. If it takes 100 or more tries to make a single human cloned embryonic stem cell line, therapeutic cloning is all but doomed as a viable future medical treatment.

Ten Million Eggs Needed

It's a simple matter of resources. There are more than 100 million Americans, according to the National Academy of Sciences [NAS], who might one day benefit from therapeutic cloning if all the high hopes for it panned out. Each therapeutic cloning attempt would require one human egg. If it takes 100 tries per patient for a cloned embryonic stem cell line to be successfully created, therapeutic cloning will never become a widely available therapy in medicine's armamentarium because there will never be enough eggs.

Do the math: 100 million patients at 100 eggs each would mean that biotechnologists would need access to at least 10 billion eggs just to treat the Americans the NAS has identified as having degenerative conditions that might respond positively to stem cell therapy. Even if we decided to strictly ration therapeutic cloning to, say, the sickest 100,000 patients, you would still need 10 million eggs! Even this strict rationing would require one million women of childbearing age to submit to egg extraction. These numbers are mind-boggling.

Is there a way out of this egg dearth? Mombaerts's article suggested two potentialities, to which I add a horrific third:

(1) Researchers could use animal eggs. Animal eggs are more readily available than human eggs, which would reduce the price of therapeutic cloning considerably. But using animal eggs would mean creating human embryos containing some non-human DNA. I doubt the American people would stand for this violation of nature's laws. (Mombaerts understates the case when he admits, "The idea of generating em-

bryos with mixed human/animal properties, even transiently, is offensive to many people.") From a practical standpoint, the stem cells and indeed all tissues that would be extracted from such human/animal hybrids would contain nonhuman mitochondrial DNA [DNA outside the egg's nucleus]. This could easily stimulate an auto-immune response or risk mitochondrial diseases in patients.

(2) Researchers might be able to learn how to transform embryonic stem cells taken from fertilized embryos into fully formed human eggs. This has been done in mice, but it will take many years to determine whether it can also be done with humans. But even if researchers learn how to morph stem cells into eggs, that does not mean they would be ready for use in cloning. Researchers would also have to ensure that they were not genetically defective and learn how to mature these eggs to the point where they would be usable for cloning. And even if they were able to learn how to do that, considering the huge number of eggs that would have to be produced in this way for therapeutic cloning to become widely available, morphing eggs out of embryonic stem cells hardly seems a plausible answer to the implacable egg dearth.

(3) Researchers could take the ovaries from female fetuses destroyed in late-term abortions, and maintain them in the hope of harvesting and maturing their eggs. I know this is revolting, but, sad to say, Dutch and Israeli researchers are already experimenting on this very thing with second- and third-trimester aborted fetuses, toward the goal of obtaining eggs for use in infertility treatments. Not only does this macabre research open the possibility that an aborted baby girl could become a mother, but if the procedure were perfected, it could result in aborted late-term female fetuses becoming a prime source of eggs for use in human cloning. As if that weren't troubling enough, the abortions of these female fetuses would have to be done in a way that did not damage

their nascent ovaries, perhaps providing utilitarian impetus for the odious partial-birth abortion technique.

Only One Logical Course of Action

To pursue therapeutic cloning is to chase a mirage. On the other hand, adult stem cell research, a practical and moral alternative to therapeutic cloning, is already in human trials and moving ahead at tremendous speed. It was just announced [2003], for example, that four out of five seriously ill human heart patients in a trial in Brazil no longer need heart transplants after being treated by their own bone marrow stem cells.

With all of the serious problems, both moral and practical, associated with human cloning, there is no longer any excuse for the current political impasse. The time has come for our senators to toss the Hatch/Feinstein phony cloning ban in the round file and pass the Brownback/Landrieu ban without further delay.

Therapeutic Cloning of Human Embryos Should Be Tolerated

Shane Ham

Shane Ham is a senior policy analyst for the Progressive Policy Institute, a research and education institute that promotes progressive politics geared to the Information Age.

Reproductive cloning is a risky and morally debatable scientific pursuit, and public fears about cloning in general stem from this ethically unsettling manner of human reproduction. Therapeutic cloning, on the other hand, does not involve bringing cloned embryos to term. Instead, therapeutic cloning utilizes stem cells from donated or discarded embryos to create new treatments for severe ailments. By using cloned cells, for example, doctors could overcome immune system reactions that have made such practices as organ and tissue transplants so problematic. Such unique and promising treatments are a worthwhile endeavor, and therefore Congress and the president should show their support for therapeutic cloning, even as they rightly continue to ban reproductive cloning.

We are living in the golden era of medical research. Almost every week a major advance is announced in the scientific journals, and [in February 2001] researchers reached a watershed in human history when they published the complete human genome, a catalog of our DNA. Despite the

Shane Ham, "The Promise of Therapeutic Cloning," *Progressive Policy Institute Backgrounder*, July 5, 2001. Reproduced by permission.

promise of breakthroughs in the near future that could help all of us lead longer and healthier lives, medical research is not immune to political pressure. The Progressive Policy Institute (PPI) [in June 2001] released a report detailing the political pressure being exerted by President [George W.] Bush to halt research into stem cells—the "universal clay" of biology that can turn into any type of tissue and potentially cure a number of diseases, from Alzheimer's to diabetes, that kill 3,000 Americans every day. Now President Bush and Republican leaders in Congress are indicating that they want to interfere with another line of research that could save millions of lives: therapeutic cloning.

It is important to distinguish between two distinct kinds of cloning: therapeutic cloning and reproductive cloning. Therapeutic cloning is not cloning in the sense most people use the term, namely using technology to create a person who is a genetically identical copy of someone else. That type of cloning is reproductive cloning, and is rightfully subject to a moratorium. Therapeutic cloning, on the other hand, seeks only to derive stem cells from a cloned embryo. The embryo is created by cloning DNA taken from a donor, which can be gathered by simply swabbing the inside of one's cheek, and transferring it into an unfertilized donor egg. The embryo then divides into a tiny clump of about 100 cells, and the stem cells are then derived to be used to create any kind of tissue, from nerve cells to arteries to organs.

Aiding Organ Transplants

The potential therapies that may be developed from therapeutic cloning are significant. Under current medical technology, patients who need organ transplants face two grave dangers: that a matching organ from a donor will not be found in time, and if an organ is found, that it will be rejected by the patient's immune system as a foreign invader. To get around the rejection risk, patients must have their immune systems suppressed, which in itself presents a grave danger, as it leaves the patient susceptible to any number of infections that people with normal immune systems do not need to worry about. (Indeed, suppression of the immune system is what makes AIDS such a lethal disease.)

Therapeutic cloning has the potential to change all of that. Since embryonic stem cells are capable of becoming any kind of tissue, researchers hope to learn to grow entire organs from scratch in a laboratory, eliminating the need to wait for organ donors. If the stem cells that create the organ are cloned from the patient, medical researchers believe that the patient's body will not recognize the organ as a foreign object; with no risk of rejection, there would be no need for dangerous immunological suppression. Therapeutic cloning, therefore, may significantly reduce the risks involved with stem cell therapies derived from non-related embryos, and save millions of lives.

The Current Ban

Federal funding for therapeutic and reproductive cloning is currently banned by the Dickey amendment, which specifies that funds cannot be used for "the creation of a human embryo or embryos for research purposes." Though this language applies to therapeutic and reproductive cloning, it is not specific to cloning; it also bans federal funding for any other methods of creating an embryo, including combining a sperm and an egg in a laboratory setting, if it is done for research purposes. In March 1997, President [Bill] Clinton extended the Dickey amendment ban on cloning [which applied to the Department of Health and Human Services (HHS)] to all federal agencies, without distinguishing between reproductive and therapeutic cloning. He also called for a voluntary moratorium on cloning by privately funded researchers. Despite the media attention surrounding the issue in the wake of Dolly, the famous sheep that was the first live clone, the National Bioethics Advisory Commission in June 1997 supported a temporary moratorium on reproductive cloning, but did not recommend against therapeutic cloning and did not recommend a permanent ban.

Many prominent scientists ... and bioethicists ... who oppose reproductive cloning still strongly favor therapeutic cloning for research based on its tremendous potential to ease human suffering.

There [have been] a number of bills in Congress that address the issue of human cloning. The House Energy and Commerce Committee's Subcommittee on Health held a hearing [in 2001] on the two leading proposals. H.R. 1644, authored by Reps. Dave Weldon (R-Fla.) and Bart Stupak (D-Mich.), would ban all human cloning under any circumstances. H.R. 2172, authored by Reps. Jim Greenwood (R-Pa.) and Peter Deutsch (D-Fla.), would ban reproductive cloning, but allow therapeutic cloning as long as researchers register with the federal government and attest to their understanding that cloned embryos are not to be implanted for pregnancy. The Greenwood-Deutsch bill would also place a ten year ban on reproductive cloning. At the hearing, HHS Deputy Secretary Claude Allen did not take a position on the two bills, but made clear that President Bush supports a total ban on all cloning. Following the hearing, House Republican Conference Chairman J.C. Watts (R-Okla.) declared a total ban on all cloning to be a top priority for the party.

An Ethical Form of Cloning

The reasons for having a moratorium on reproductive cloning are fairly clear. Changing the way humans have reproduced for millions of years raises a host of ethical questions which society is only now beginning to consider. Moreover, reproductive cloning is still an unproven and extremely unsafe technique. Though a small number of animals have been successfully cloned, for every clone that is born there are dozens more unsuccessful clones that are either miscarried or seriously malformed. It is unclear at this stage whether even those "successful" clones are truly successful; there is evidence to suggest that cloned organisms suffer from significant developmental and health problems. The temporary moratorium on reproductive cloning, therefore, is entirely appropriate.

Therapeutic cloning, on the other hand, does not engender the same safety and ethical concerns. While therapeutic cloning does involve the creation of an embryo, the derivation of stem cells from cloned embryos is the same as the derivation from leftover embryos, and any cloned human embryos would be created with the express permission of the donor and the express understanding that the embryo would be used for stem cell derivation only, not for implantation. Many prominent scientists (such as Rudolf Jaenisch) and bioethicists (such as Arthur L. Caplan) who oppose reproductive cloning still strongly favor therapeutic cloning for research based on its tremendous potential to ease human suffering.

What Should Be Done

Some critics of therapeutic cloning contend that the temptation to implant cloned embryos will be too great, and the birth of a human clone would be inevitable. The Greenwood-Deutsch legislation addresses that concern by providing severe criminal penalties—up to 10 years in prison—for researchers who implant embryonic clones. This safeguard should be sufficient to deter those who can be deterred; for those who are determined to create a human clone despite the legal impediments, even a total ban on creating embryonic clones will not stop them. (And no ban passed by Congress can stop scientists in other countries from reproductive cloning.) The potential reward in advanced therapies for dreaded diseases more than justifies the risk.

Though cloning is still a new science and caution is warranted, there is no need to close off a promising avenue of scientific inquiry because of justified fears of reproductive cloning. Therefore, PPI recommends the following steps to let this vital research go forward:

1. Congress should pass, and President Bush should sign, the Greenwood-Deutsch bill (H.R. 2172) to ban reproductive cloning for 10 years. . . . [this bill never left the Senate]

2. President Bush should revise the executive ban on federal funding for cloning to allow funding for therapeutic cloning while continuing to ban funding for reproductive cloning. When President Clinton issued his order barring federal agencies from supporting human cloning, he acted out of prudent intent to slow the scientists until bioethicists and policymakers had a chance to consider the implications of cloning. In the accompanying legislation Clinton sent to Congress, he asked for a five-year sunset period on the ban in order to force reconsideration of cloning when more information was available. . . . With legal prohibitions and funding bans firmly in place against reproductive cloning, there is no reason to continue the ban on federal funds for research into therapeutic cloning.

3. Congress should repeal the Dickey amendment and allow HHS and the National Institutes of Health (NIH) to fund research in therapeutic cloning. While Clinton's ban extended the Dickey amendment to all agencies, repealing that ban would not benefit researchers unless the Dickey amendment is repealed. The primary source of funding for biomedical research is NIH, a division of HHS, and the Dickey amendment is a rider on the HHS appropriations bill. To ensure that scientists have the resources they need to conduct their important research, the Dickey amendment must be repealed. NIH could then change their guidelines to allow funding for research using stem cells derived from embryos created through asexual cloning for research purposes (somatic nuclear

transfer), while still confining funding for research on stem-cells derived from embryos created sexually (by combining eggs with sperm) to those derived from excess in vitro fertilization embryos which would otherwise be discarded.

It is entirely appropriate to be skeptical about powerful new technologies, and to take a collective pause to consider the next step. The United States did so with cloning. But now that we have a clearer picture of the risks and a firm understanding that reproductive cloning should not take place now, if ever, we should move forward cautiously with therapeutic cloning to see if it can live up to its promise. . . . We must not close the door on this important medical research because of fears about reproductive cloning. With [hoped for legal] safeguards . . . and the oversight inherent in federal funding, research into therapeutic cloning can go forward under the bright light of public scrutiny and perhaps, one day in the future, save lives.

13

Embryonic Stem Cell Research Threatens Women's Health

Pia de Solenni

Pia de Solenni is a Catholic theologian and director of life and women's issues at the Family Research Council, a public policy group that promotes Judeo-Christian views on faith, the family, and American society.

Advocates of therapeutic cloning emphasize how this form of embryonic stem cell research can help millions who suffer from disease and illness. What these supporters fail to mention, however, is that tens of millions or even hundreds of millions of women would be needed to provide enough embryo cells to overcome the estimated 1-in-100 success ratio of embryonic stem cell treatments. Furthermore, entailed in this staggering harvest is the painful and occasionally fatal process of increasing donor women's ovulation. Because these negative aspects are often ignored, it is likely that few have considered how therapeutic cloning would exploit women and increase the risks to women's health worldwide.

The U.S. Congress is poised to pour unlimited funds into embryonic stem cell research that not only destroys innocent human life, but it has shown no substantial promise as a curative and threatens the health of women worldwide. So much for "progress and advancement."

After more than 20 years, embryonic stem cell research has not yielded a single cure. During this same time, adult stem cells have been used to treat people with heart disease, Parkinson's disease, spinal cord injuries and at least 50 other documented conditions.

Women's Forgotten Roles

The focus on therapeutic cloning has been aimed at our heartstrings, prophesying cures for our loved ones, friends, and even movie stars. But scientists, politicians, and academics have all turned a blind eye to the women who will be affected. After all, embryonic stem cell research depends upon millions of embryos. Whether created through *in vitro* fertilization or somatic cell nuclear transfer (cloning), each embryo requires a woman's egg in order to be created. Theoretically, embryonic stem cell research would allow each patient to receive specialized treatment to avoid rejection complications similar to those caused by organ transplants.

Let's take the example of just one disease. In the U.S., there are 17 million diabetes patients. In a report on therapeutic cloning in mice published in the 2003 *Proceedings of the National Academy of Sciences USA*, scientist Peter M[o]mbaerts found that, based on cloning experiment[s] done in mice, if the same model could be developed for human cloning, each cure for each patient would require 10–100 human eggs. M[o]mbaerts puts the cost at $100,000–200,000 per patient. To treat the 17 million American diabetes patients, we would need 170 million–1.7 billion human eggs.

Women have . . . died from egg harvesting.

On average, a woman undergoing hyper ovarian stimulation releases 10–12 eggs per treatment. In other words, somewhere between 17 million and 170 million women would be required to donate their eggs. According to the 2000 census, there are about 60 million American women of reproductive age. We can hardly assume that all 60 million American women would be willing to donate their eggs; so, mathematically speaking, there would have to be donors from outside of the U.S. to make up for the additional eggs required to treat the disease just among Americans.

Millions of Women Donors Required

The 2004 South Korean cloning of a human being [which proved to be an untrue claim] required 242 eggs for one stem cell line. For 17 million patients, that means 4,114,000,000 human eggs, about 400 million women donors.

Dr. David Prentice, Professor of Life Sciences, at Indiana State University, now at the Family Research Council, cites a 2005 South Korean report in which the average stem cell line required 17 eggs. For diabetes, that means 289 million eggs. If we follow Dr. Prentice's model, we would need about 29 million women donors.

Regardless of which model we follow, the reality is that millions of women will be required to provide eggs. Women whose eggs are harvested undergo a long, uncomfortable, painful and potentially dangerous process called ovarian hyperstimulation. Some of the drugs used have never been approved for this use by the FDA [Food and Drug Administration]. Complications from the procedure include a potential link to ovarian cysts and cancers, severe pelvic pain, rupture of the ovaries, stroke, possible negative effects on future fertility, and even death.

In clinical studies using Pergonal for ovarian hyperstimulation, 2.4–5.5 percent of women developed complications. If we're talking about 29 million women, that means at least 696,000 of them would develop complications. Over 100,000 would be classified as severe cases.

Women have also died from egg harvesting. Knowing this, most women would not consent to egg harvesting unless they felt they had no choice. These women could be described as those needing money, typically poor women, students, and/or women from developing countries. Such women are not in a position to give informed consent because their financial need impairs their ability to adequately weigh the risks involved.

Endorsing any form of legislation supporting embryonic stem cell research means putting thousands of women at risk of serious illness, disability, or even death. One would hope that an advanced and progressive country would treat its women better than that.

14

Women Should Be Well Paid When Donating Eggs for Embryonic Research

Ronald M. Green

Ronald M. Green is a professor of Ethics and Human Values at Dartmouth College and the director of the college's Institute for the Study of Applied and Professional Ethics. He is the author of many articles and five books in the fields of ethical theory, religious ethics, and applied ethics, including medical ethics and business ethics.

Egg donors are needed to provide the stem cells used in embryonic research. These women should be fairly compensated for their time and willingness to take part in this burgeoning but uncertain field. After all, participants in other risky medical experiments are well paid for their contributions. Yet many state statutes prohibit compensation for eggs beyond a token fee. These payment restrictions must be eliminated. If they are not, fewer women will want to become donors, and the crucial field of embryonic research will suffer.

R ecent initiatives around the country give new impetus to stem-cell research, including California's Proposition 71 and a similar measure in Massachusetts. Prompted by these developments, the National Academy of Sciences issued model guidelines in April [2005] for institutions sponsoring stem-cell research.

Ronald M. Green, "It's Right to Pay Women Who Give Their Eggs for Research," *San Francisco Chronicle*, July 19, 2005. Reproduced by permission of the author.

Unfortunately, these laudable guidelines prohibit payment for human eggs beyond out-of-pocket expenses for the donors. This prohibition threatens to shut down two of the most important branches of stem-cell research: therapeutic cloning and parthenogenesis. Therapeutic cloning involves inserting a donor's cell nucleus into an egg that has had its nucleus removed. Parthenogenesis involves direct stimulation of an egg to develop and yield a supply of stem cells that either match the DNA of the egg donor or can be closely matched to other recipients. Both technologies could lead to the creation of an abundant supply of tissues and even whole organs, such as kidneys, without the need to suppress the recipient's immune system with drugs.

Just Compensation

What is the point of these bans against paying for eggs? A ban on payment for embryos makes sense. Embryos that are available for stem-cell research are spares remaining from in-vitro fertilization procedures. Whatever effort or expense went into them lies in the past. It also makes sense to prohibit the selling of sperm for research purposes. This is hardly an onerous or risky task.

But eggs are another matter. Eggs should not be sold, but women who produce eggs for research should be compensated for the time and effort involved. They must undergo a series of painful injections with drugs to stimulate their ovaries and undergo a collection procedure that involves inserting a large needle through the vaginal wall into each ovary. The drugs can cause mood swings, and there are rare but life-threatening risks associated with them. Why would anybody do this without appropriate compensation?

Some believe that women should be protected from such risks. But our society has already concluded that women may undertake them for a good reason. Throughout the United States, women are allowed to serve as reproductive egg donors to help other women have children. Infertility clinics around the country routinely compensate reproductive egg donors for the discomfort and inconvenience involved. They have found that without payment, few women step forward even to assist other women have children. At this moment, Great Britain, which bans payment for reproductive egg donors, is reconsidering its rules, as more and more British couples go abroad for treatment.

Payment Bans Will Hinder Progress

But if payment for reproductive egg donation is morally acceptable, why is it wrong to compensate women for the discomfort and time associated with the donation of tissue to lifesaving research? The rationale for this ban becomes even murkier when we consider that human participants in other painful or risky research are usually paid. Federal regulations permit such payments as long as they do not constitute an "undue influence" that distorts free and informed consent. If the validity of the consent process is ensured and payment levels are kept reasonable, why are women treated as though they cannot make these decisions themselves?

I serve as chairman of the Ethics Advisory Board for Massachusetts-based Advanced Cell Technology. For the past four years, ACT has conducted pioneering research on therapeutic cloning. It is also a leader in parthenogenesis research. To conduct this research, ACT has used human eggs provided through an ethically responsible egg-donor program. This program pays research egg donors who have been carefully screened for medical and psychological vulnerabilities and who have met various criteria set out to minimize the risk. Payment is set at the same rates as reproductive egg donors in the New England region. We have found that women who donate eggs are motivated both by monetary and altruistic considerations, but that they are unlikely to consider undertaking this onerous procedure if there is not some compensation for the effort and discomfort associated with it.

Those who have proposed bans on payments for egg donors seek to protect women. They also want to foster stem-cell research. But women's freedom and the progress of stem-cell research will both be hindered if these bans go into effect. We must respect a woman's decision to be an egg donor by reasonably compensating her, which will benefit both her and the progress of this crucial science.

Organizations to Contact

The editors have compiled the following list of organizations concerned with the issues debated in this book. The descriptions are derived from materials provided by the organizations. All have publications or information available for interested readers. The list was compiled on the date of publication of the present volume; the information provided here may change. Be aware that many organizations take several weeks or longer to respond to inquiries, so allow as much time as possible.

**American Association for the Advancement
of Science (AAAS)**
1200 New York Ave. NW, Washington, DC   20005
(202) 326-6400
e-mail: webmaster@aaas.org
Web site: www.aaas.org

The AAAS is an international organization with the goal of advancing scientific inquiry worldwide. The AAAS provides a forum for educators, students, and the general public to learn more about the possibilities of emerging sciences. On the topic of embryonic experimentation, the AAAS promotes ethical research practices with hopes that those suffering from debilitating diseases will benefit from the findings. The journal *Science* is the publication of the AAAS, and the Web site EurekAlert.org provides breaking science news from around the globe.

American Life League (ALL)
PO Box 1350, Stafford, VA   22555
(540) 659-4171 • fax: (540) 659-2586
e-mail: info@all.org
Web site: www.all.org

ALL is a pro-life organization dedicated to promoting ideals and government policies that preserve the sanctity of all human life. The group is openly and adamantly opposed to abortion, embryonic stem cell research, and birth control. ALL publishes the magazine *Celebrate Life*, provides tips and opportunities for individuals who are interested in aiding in advancing the pro-life cause, and sponsors numerous organizations and events that aid in educating the public about pro-life practices.

Center for Bioethics and Human Dignity (CBHD)
2065 Half Day Rd., Bannockburn, IL   60015
(847) 317-8180 • fax: (847) 317-8101
e-mail: info@cbhd.org
Web site: www.cbhd.org

The CBHD investigates ethical issues of emerging biotechnology from a Christian perspective. The center publishes position statements and overviews on many issues including cloning, reproductive ethics, and stem cell research. In the position statement on stem cell research, the center provides ethical, legal, and scientific objections to the practices of embryonic stem cell research that kill the embryo in order to harvest stem cells. The organization sponsors many conferences each year concerning bioethics.

Coalition for the Advancement of Medical Research (CAMR)
2021 K St. NW, Suite 305, Washington, DC   20006
(202) 293-2856
e-mail: CAMResearch@yahoo.com
Web site: www.camradvocacy.org

CAMR is a coalition of organizations that support continued research of embryonic stem cells. Members of CAMR include patient groups, universities, and scientific societies. The coalition's Web site provides extensive information on the curative potential of embryonic stem cells and the need for increased funding.

Do No Harm: The Coalition of Americans for Research Ethics

1100 H St. NW, Suite 700, Washington, DC   20005
(202) 347-6840 • fax: (202) 347-6849
Web site: www.stemcellresearch.org

Do No Harm is an organization that promotes medical research and treatment that does not result in the destruction of human life or human embryos. The organization promotes adult stem cell research as a viable alternative to embryonic stem cell research. The group has published numerous fact sheets, and its Web site contains links to news and commentary on stem cell research.

The Hastings Center

21 Malcolm Gordon Rd., Garrison, NY   10524
(845) 424-4040 • fax: (845) 424-4545
e-mail: mail@thehastingscenter.org
Web site: www.thehastingscenter.org

The Hastings Center is a nonprofit organization that examines the ethical issues surrounding current biotechnology advancements. Its interdisciplinary teams present a range of viewpoints on select topics. The center publishes two bimonthly journals concerning bioethics, *The Hastings Center Report* and *IRB: Ethics and Human Research.*

Human Cloning Foundation (HCF)

PMB 143, 1100 Hammond Dr., Suite 410A
Atlanta, GA   30328
e-mail: contactus@humancloning.org
Web site: www.humancloning.org

HCF is a nonprofit organization dedicated to advancing human cloning and other related biotechnology practices, including human embryo experimentation. The group believes that through further research and practice, human cloning could potentially cure numerous diseases. The HCF Web site provides fact sheets and testimonials related to the benefits and myths of human cloning.

International Society for Stem Cell Research (ISSCR)
60 Revere Dr., Suite 500, Northbrook, IL   60062
(847) 509-1944 • fax: (847) 480-9282
e-mail: isscr@isscr.org
Web site: www.isscr.org

In promoting the advancement of stem cell research, ISSCR seeks to accurately inform the public about the possibilities and goals of this research. The society encourages ethical embryonic research in hopes that its findings will yield treatment for many, otherwise incurable diseases. The ISSCR has openly opposed and lobbied against U.S. and U.N. bans on embryonic stem cell research. Educational materials are available for the public on the organization's Web site.

The President's Council on Bioethics
1801 Pennsylvania Ave. NW, Suite 700
Washington, DC   20006
(202) 296-4669
e-mail: info@bioethics.gov
Web site: www.bioethics.gov

President George W. Bush established the President's Council on Bioethics in November 2001 as the primary presidential advisory committee on bioethical issues. The council is responsible for evaluating topics such as stem cell research, cloning, and reproductive technologies. The reports produced by the council are intended to assist in the governmental decision- making process on biotechnological issues and inform the public on these topics. Reports by the council are available online.

National Right to Life Committee [NRLC]
512 10th St. NW, Washington, DC   20004
(202) 626-8800
e-mail: nrlc@nrlc.org
Web site: www.nrlc.org

The NRLC was founded following the decision of the U.S. Supreme Court case *Roe vs. Wade*, which federally legalized abortion. The organization acts as a lobbying group that promotes a pro-life government agenda, including advocating for a ban on nontherapeutic human embryo experimentation. The NRLC publishes the monthly *National Right to Life News*.

Snowflakes Embryo Adoption Program
Nightlight Christian Adoptions, Fullerton, CA   92831
(714) 278-1020 • fax: (714) 278-1063
e-mail: info@Nightlight.org
Web site: www.snowflakes.org

As one branch of Nightlight Christian Adoptions, Snowflakes Embryo Adoption Program focuses on finding couples to adopt and carry to term frozen embryos that would otherwise be discarded by fertility clinics. The program promotes the idea that life begins at conception, and that embryos are pre-born children that deserve the opportunity to live a healthy life.

Society for Developmental Biology (SDB)
9650 Rockville Pike, Bethesda, MD   20814
(301) 571-0647 • fax: (301) 571-5704
Web site: www.sdbonline.org

SDB is a global organization that was founded in 1939 with the mission of promoting increased research in the field of developmental biology. Members of the SDB have supported a voluntary moratorium on human cloning. Regarding the issue of therapeutic cloning, the SDB Board of Trustees believes only limited knowledge can be gained by researching only existing stem cell lines as outlined by the Bush administration's federal policy. It supports the creation of a new oversight committee to address bioethical concerns in the United States.

Stem Cell Research Foundation (SCRF)
22512 Gateway Center Dr., Clarksburg, MD   20871
(877) 842-3442
e-mail: info@stemcellresearchfoundation.org
Web site: www.stemcellresearchfoundation.org

The SCRF is an organization dedicated to advancing stem cell therapies by providing research grants to organizations in the field. The foundation sees great promise in the ability of stem cell therapy to treat disease and find lasting cures. Publications such as *Stem Cell Research: A Revolution in Medicine* and *The Source* are available online.

Bibliography

Books

Michael Bellomo

The Stem Cell Divide: The Facts, the Fiction, and the Fear Driving the Greatest Scientific, Political and Religious Debate of Our Time. New York: American Management Association, 2006.

Ronald M. Green

The Human Embryo Research Debates: Bioethics in the Vortex of Controversy. New York: Oxford University Press, 2001.

Suzanne Holland, Karen Lebacqz, and Laurie Zoloth, eds.

The Human Embryonic Stem Cell Debate: Science, Ethics and Public Policy. Cambridge, MA: MIT Press, 2001.

Leon R. Kass

Life, Liberty, and the Defense of Dignity: The Challenge for Bioethics. Washington, DC: AEI, 2002.

Ann A. Kiessling and Scott Anderson

Human Embryonic Stem Cells: An Introduction to the Science and Therapeutic Potential. Boston: Jones and Bartlett, 2003.

Jane Maienschein

Whose View of Life? Embryos, Cloning, and Stem Cells. Cambridge, MA: Harvard University Press, 2003.

Joseph Panno

Stem Cell Research: Medical Applications and Ethical Controversy. New York: Facts On File, 2005.

Ann B. Parson   *The Proteus Effect: Stem Cells and Their Promise for Medicine.* Washington, DC: Joseph Henry, 2004.

Gregory E. Pence   *Who's Afraid of Human Cloning?* Lanham, MD: Rowman & Littlefield, 1998.

David A. Prentice   *Stem Cells and Cloning.* San Francisco: Benjamin Cummings, 2003.

President's Council on Bioethics   *Human Cloning and Human Dignity: The Report of the President's Council on Bioethics.* New York: Public Affairs, 2002.

Christopher Thomas Scott   *Stem Cell Now: From the Experiment that Shook the World to the New Politics of Life.* New York: Pi, 2006.

Nancy E. Snow, ed.   *Stem Cell Research: New Frontiers in Science and Ethics.* Notre Dame, IN: University of Notre Dame Press, 2003.

Pam Solo and Gail Pressberg   *The Promise and Politics of Stem Cell Research.* Westport, CT: Praeger, 2006.

Brent Waters and Ronald Cole-Turner, eds.   *God and the Embryo: Religious Voices on Stem Cells and Cloning.* Washington, DC: Georgetown University Press, 2003.

Periodicals

Dave Andrusko — "No Human Embryos Created or Destroyed: Embryonic Stem Cells Created from Skin Cell," *National Right to Life News*, September 2005.

Ronald Bailey — "Is Heaven Populated Chiefly by the Souls of Embryos?" *Reason* Online, December 22, 2004. www.reason.com.

Charles Q. Choi — "Blastomere Blowup," *Scientific American*, November 2006.

Eric Cohen — "Go Forth and Replicate: The Age of Human Cloning Has Arrived," *Weekly Standard*, May 30, 2005.

Eric Cohen and William Kristol — "Frist's Stem Cell Capitulation," *Weekly Standard*, August 8, 2005.

Jon Cohen — "Stem Cell Pioneers," *Smithsonian*, December 2005.

Michael Ennis — "Culture of Strife," *Texas Monthly*, October 2005.

Sharon Gunderson — "Stem Cell Institute May Boost Local Economy," *San Diego Business Journal*, March 28, 2005.

Stan Guthrie — "Worth Protecting," *Christianity Today*, November 2006.

Mathew Herper and Robert Langreth — "Anti-ban Billionaires," *Forbes Global*, September 4, 2006.

Josephine Johnston	"Paying Egg Donors: Exploring the Arguments," *Hastings Center Report*, January–February 2006.
John F. Kavanaugh	"Cloning, by Whatever Name, Smells Bad: 'We Must Offer a Positive Alternative,'" *America*, June 19, 2006.
Robert Klitzman and Joseph Siragusa	"Contexts, Anyone?: The Need for Contextualization in the Debate About the Moral Status of Embryos," *American Journal of Bioethics*, November–December 2005.
Tenneille Ludwig	"Human Embryonic Stem Cells: The View from the Lab Bench," *Milwaukee Journal Sentinel*, September 3, 2006.
Zubin Master	"Can We Really Bypass the Moral Debate for Embryo Research?" *American Journal of Bioethics*, November–December 2005.
Ryan M. McCaffrey	"Stem Cell Research and Natural Law," *Harvard Salient*, October 26, 2006.
Carolyn McLeod	"Embryo Autonomy? What about the Autonomy of Infertility Patients," *American Journal of Bioethics*, November–December 2005.
Liza Mundy	"Souls on Ice," *Mother Jones*, July–August 2006.
David S. Oderberg	"Human Embryonic Stem Cell Research: What's Wrong with It?" *Human Life Review*, Fall 2005.

Frank Rich   "The Passion of the Embryos," *New York Times*, July 23, 2006.

Christine A.   "Ethics Interrupted," *Christianity To-*
Scheller   *day*, October 2005.

Patricia Schudy   "An Embryo by Any Other Name?" *National Catholic Reporter*, August 26, 2005.

David A. Shaywitz "Cell Out," *Wall Street Journal*, July 26, 2006.

Peter Singer   "The Sanctity of Life," *Foreign Policy*, September–October 2005.

Wesley J. Smith   "Demolishing Anti-Life Propaganda: A Stem Cell Tale," *National Right to Life News*, January 2005.

Wesley J. Smith   "The Great Stem Cell Coverup: Promising Medical Research You Never Hear About," *Weekly Standard*, August 7, 2006.

David van Gend   "Prometheus, Pandora, and the Myths of Cloning," *The Human Life Review*, Summer–Fall 2006.

David Wasserman "What Qualifies as a Live Embryo?" *American Journal of Bioethics*, November–December 2005.

Rick Weiss   "The Power to Divide: Stem Cells," *National Geographic*, July 2005.

Index

A

Abortion opponents, 31, 43–45
Adult stem cell research
    funding of, 59
    potential of, 16–18, 27
    progress in, 19–20, 52
Adult stem cells
    vs. embryonic stem cells, 7–8,
    11–12, 51
    limits of, 14
Advanced Cell Technology (ACT),
    80
Allen, Claude, 70
Alzheimer's disease, 8
America, 50
American Association for the Advancement of Science (AAAS),
    82
American Life League (ALL),
    82–83
Animal eggs, 64–65
Animal research, 8

B

Baldacci, John, 47
Bans
    on cloning, is needed, 61–66
    on paying egg donors, 78–81
    on stem cell research, violates
    human rights, 42–45
Beckwith, Frank, 23–24
Belgium, 58
Berger, Sam, 46
Bilateral symmetry, 34–35
Biotechnology Industry Organization, 62
Birth defects, 13

Blair, Tony, 26
Blastomeres, 37
Britain, 58
Bush, George W.
    on human cloning, 62, 70
    stem cell research policy of,
    7–8, 9, 58–59, 68

C

California, 50–52, 57, 78
Catholic Church, 43
Cavitation, 36, 37
Cell differentiation, 15, 17–18
Center for Bioethics and Human
    Dignity (CBHD), 83
Chemical screening, 13
Clinton, Bill, 58, 69
Cloning
    process of, 22–23
    reproductive, 23, 68–71
    restrictions on, 58
    should be banned, 61–66
    therapeutic vs. reproductive,
    23, 68
    See also Therapeutic cloning
Coalition for the Advancement of
    Medical Research (CAMR), 83
Compaction, 36, 37
Crist, Charles, 47–48
Culver, Chet, 47
Cures
    from adult stem cell therapies,
    19–20
    from embryonic stem cell
    therapies, 8, 13, 14
    potential for, is exaggerated,
    16–20